PLAYS BY
JACK GILHOOLEY

BROADWAY PLAY PUBLISHING INC
224 E 62nd St, NY, NY 10065
www.broadwayplaypub.com
info@broadwayplaypub.com

PLAYS BY JACK GILHOOLEY
© Copyright 2006 by Jack Gilhooley

Cover photo by Bill Wisser

First printing: July 2006
This printing: August 2016
I S B N: 978-0-88145-275-4

Book design: Marie Donovan
Word processing: Microsoft Word
Typographic controls: Xerox Ventura Publisher 2.0 P E
Typeface: Palatino
Printed and bound in the U S A

CONTENTS

ABOUT THE AUTHOR

Jack Gilhooley is a proud alumnus of New Dramatists and the Eugene O'Neill Theater Center (Connecticut). He has been awarded two N E A grants (Individual Artist and International), four Florida State Artists grants and a New York Foundation for the Arts Fellowship (CONNEMARA DREAMING). In 2004-05, he was the initial recipient of the John Ringling Fund Artists Fellowship for GULF WARS. He has twice been named a Fulbright guest artist and has been faculty at University de Salamanca in Spain and Mount Holyoke College among others and has served as guest artist and lecturer at universities and theaters throughout America and in Canada and Ireland. Partially funded by the Puffin Foundation, RED BESSIE (co-author, Daniel Czitrom) was widely heralded at the 2003 Edinburgh Festival. The two-hander with songs about beleaguered American troubadours from the Spanish Civil War to the Cold War was described by *London Times* critic, Keith Miller as "clear-headed and humane, not unaware of the hurt that political idealism can cause, and more fun than might be expected of such a high-minded project." He has twice been commissioned by Actors Theater of Louisville and by Earplay and American Playhouse. Hes been awarded grants and/or fellowships from the Shubert Foundation, PEN, the Carnegie Fund, the Pilgrim Project, Canada Council and five of his plays have been produced with developmental funding from the Ford Foundation. He's been a guest playwright at the Carnegie Mellon Showcase of New Plays, the Aspen Festival, the Sundance Playwrights Lab, Mount Sequoyah New Play Retreat, North Carolina New Playwrights Festival, and the Avignon Festival. His plays have been presented or workshopped at major theaters around the country and at Circle Rep, The Phoenix, N Y S F, Manhattan Theater Club, Theater For the New City, on Theater Row and at many other venues in New York. Guest artist residencies include Yaddo, the Millay Colony, the MacDowell Colony, the Dorset Playwrights Colony, the Djerassi and the Edward Albee Foundations, the Tyrone Guthrie International Institute (Ireland) and Hawthornden Castle (Scotland). His Joseph Papp-produced play, THE TIME TRIAL (with Tommy Lee Jones) was London-optioned and published by Broadway Play Publishing Inc in *Plays From The New York Shakespeare Festival*. Raised in upper Manhattan, then Philadelphia, Gilhooley is married to writer-dramatist, Jo Morello.

MUMMERS

ACKNOWLEDGMENTS

For support with the development of MUMMERS, thanks to New Dramatists; the Folger Theater Group, Washington DC, Louis Scheeder, producer and director; as well as Jean Barker, Marie Wallace, Frederic Warriner, John LaGioia, Mary Carney, Joseph Sullivan, Anne Stone and John Gilliss.

for the memory of Bob Gilhooley, a loyal Mummerfile,
and for Peter Maloney

CHARACTERS & SETTING

SHOOTER O'ROURKE, *an octogenarian, slowing down a bit lately but still a heller*

SPIKE O'ROURKE, *his son, early sixties. Just a shadow of his old man*

COOKIE O'ROURKE, SPIKE's *wife. Pleasantly eccentric at her best but genuinely mad in her darker moments. An Irish immigrant who has retained her brogue*

PEACHES O'ROURKE CATANIA, *their daughter, a dazzling forty-ish (then twenty-five years later)*

GASPARI "HOAGIE" CATANIA, PEACHES's *husband, a forty-five-ish successful lawyer (then twenty-five years later)*

TRIXIE CATANIA, *their daughter, a pretty U of Pennsylvania co-ed (then chic middle-aged)*

FRANCIS JOSEPH "FRANJO" CATANIA , *their son, seventeen*

DENISE WALKER , *an African-American T V newscaster. Pretty, charming, an Afro in her twenties* and *a contemporary hair style in middle-age*

BARRY , a T V cameraman

*BUDDY O'ROURKE , *a memory appearing only to* COOKIE. *Her son, killed at nineteen in the early days of Vietnam*

**double cast (suggested)*

Time: The play takes (primarily) between Christmas and January 1, 1976 and on the cusp of the 21st century

Place: The basement den of a row house in the blue-collar neighborhood of Kensington in North Philadelphia

All of the music and video material can be obtained from the Mummers Museum, 1100 S 2nd St, Philadelphia, PA 19147, 215 336-3050, fax 215 389-5630.

dedicated to Jo

ACT ONE

(The play opens in darkness. A film clip from the traditional Philadelphia New Year's Day Mummers parade flashes on a screen above the set or on a back wall. As the curtain rises—or as the audience enters—we should hear some authentic string band music with particular emphasis on the mummer's theme, Oh Dem Golden Slippers. *The film should run long enough for an uninitiated audience to get a feel for the annual event. Underneath the screen with arms outstretched, four caped male figures do the Mummer's "strut" in darkness. One seems absolutely ancient, another aged and perhaps portly, a third in the prime of life and the fourth, seemingly a youth.)*

(Into the midst of their revelry marches a young, decorated soldier. He'll be pinspotted and he'll have a military demeanor. The strutters will lift him onto their shoulders as they would a returning hero. He will absolutely glow with pride and salute as all fades out.)

(A long moment in darkness. Then a spot up on DENISE *who is out of the stage picture and off to one side as a well-dressed, black, attractive, forty-plus, present-day commentator. She's the only one not in a "freeze". Three other characters are in semi-darkness in Christmastime, 1975.* TRIXIE *stands at the open back door of the basement den of her grandparent's row house, angrily ready to exit. Her mother,* PEACHES *and her grandmother,* COOKIE *stare intently at her. They are laboring over what appears to be two fabulous and outrageous costumes [red, white and blue]. Throughout the room is an impressive array of plaques, trophies, photo blow-ups and mementoes of parades gone by including a glass-enclosed case with an old-time tramp's outfit. An ancient pistol is on the top of the case in a holder. In the center of the room is a banner reading, "Brotherly Love Mummer's Club".)*

(Aside from these accoutrements and a lighted Christmas tree, the room seems a conventional, renovated basement den with a T V, small bar, etc. including an inconspicuous statue of The Virgin.)

DENISE: It was late 1975. I was new to Philadelphia, reluctantly aware that my opportunities were greater in media than on stage. Well, not *greater*. More abundant for a woman of color. I'd spent three years in unpaid, unappreciated New York hardscrabble theater. All I'd gained was an insight. The arts—theater in particular—had no more tolerance than the rest of America. Often less. And I had yet to realize that I just might be a limited performer.
   And so I jumped on the bandwagon of American liberal guilt. I was overpaid and under prepared. But willing. And young and fueled by pride.

I'd report on community affairs in a city approaching blackness. I'd submitted a list of topics focused on the problems and achievements of my people. But T V-logic reared its empty head. A nice young member of my women's group wrote to the station requesting that I cover her family. They were white ethnics preparing to celebrate that very dubious aspect of themselves. *(Subdued)* Hurrah!

(Spot out on DENISE. *Lights up on the set)*

*(*TRIXIE *absolutely slams on her exit. Both remaining women stare at the door.)*

COOKIE: *(Brogue)* Goin' through a phase, she is.

PEACHES: It's natural.

COOKIE: Every girl says it at her age.

PEACHES: I did.

COOKIE: You did.

PEACHES: *You* did.

COOKIE: I *didn't.*

PEACHES: You just said...every girl says it at her age.

COOKIE: But I'd already met yer da'.

PEACHES: Even after I met Gaspari I kept sayin', "I'll never marry." I'd say it even though I knew he was the one.

COOKIE: He was the *one* arright. Even as ya said it you were in a family way.

PEACHES: Ma!!!

COOKIE: *(Quietly)* I *hope* he was the one.

PEACHES: Mother!!!

COOKIE: Well, it's O K. Everythin' worked out. Good husband. Good father.

PEACHES: We did the right thing...the honorable thing.

COOKIE: If ya did the right thing, you wouldn'ta had to do the honorable thing.

PEACHES: Enough!

COOKIE: I'm not castin' aspersions. It's fashionable nowadays. Youngsters are freer... more...liberated. That's the word?

PEACHES: Uninhibited.

COOKIE: *(Nods)* Dirtier. Nowadays, lots go to the altar with a bun in the oven. If they go at all. But in the fifties, you two were like...pioneers... trailblazers, you were. You were...*stupid.*

PEACHES: *(Patiently trying to end this)* We were progressive thinkers.

COOKIE: Thinkin' had nothin' t'do with it. Anyway, Trixie will meet the right boy. She has to have a kid.

PEACHES: She's only nineteen. Let 'er breathe.

COOKIE: If she don't... *(Snapping her fingers awkwardly)* ...poof! There goes the record.

PEACHES: We got the record. And nobody's closin' in.

COOKIE: *(Pause)* Colored people could break it. They break alla the records, nowadays.

PEACHES: There are no "colored people".

COOKIE: *(Incredulously)* No colored people??? In Philly? You been out there in your Main Line, split-level ranch house too long. You're outta touch.

PEACHES: *(Exasperated) In the parade* there are no "colored people".

COOKIE: Oh, yeah. But someday...

PEACHES: Long after we've forgotten about the record.

COOKIE: I'll never forget about the record. Coloreds reproduce. They could have a five-year-old mummer, his twenty-five-year-old daddy, his forty-five-year-old granddaddy, his sixty-five-year-old great-granddaddy and his eighty-five-year-old great-great-granddaddy. Five generations! We're blockbusted. That's why Trixie hasta marry...have a little mummer. Soon's he starts t'toddle we put him inna parade. Five generations. We'd be inna Guiness Book of Records. *(Beat)* I never been inna book before.

PEACHES: You're in the phone book.

COOKIE: Under yer grandfather. *(Muses)* Yeah, unbreakable. We'd be like Babe Ruth.

PEACHES: His records are broken. The real big one by a colored man.

COOKIE: Nothin's sacred. Maybe we need six generations. *(Beat)* We'll never get six. No way, like the kids say.

PEACHES: You sound like grandpa's about to keel over.

COOKIE: He's an octogenarian.

PEACHES: He doesn't act it.

COOKIE: He doesn't act like he *knows* it.
We matter. Feature stories inna papers. We're gonna be on T V.

PEACHES: The entire parade's on T V. And we got the record on a technicality.

COOKIE: Y'mean, cause Gaspari's not an O'Rourke? That's legit. The committee voted. They said that Gaspari Catania could take Buddy O'Rourke's place cause he was a brother-in-law? What was t'be done? You think the commies were gonna let Buddy come home from North Vietnam t'do the "Mummer's Strut"? Gaspari's only substitutin' for your brother. The war's over. When Buddy gets released, he'll march for himself.

(PEACHES *is profoundly disturbed but unable to reproach Cookie. Quietly...*)

PEACHES: Well...maybe you shouldn't depend...maybe you're expectin' too much. I dunno if you're bein' realistic about Buddy.

COOKIE: The lad'll march. He knows he was fightin' for things like the Mummers parade. Highly decorated, your little brother. Don't ever forget that, Peaches.

PEACHES: I never do, Ma.

COOKIE: I gotta feelin' about this year, Peaches. Like it's special.

PEACHES: You have a special feelin' every year, Ma.

COOKIE: I hope he doesn't come home speakin' Vietnam. I wonder if ya spend enough time with 'em, you develop...y'know, gook features.

(*Lost in her own thoughts, she "slants" her eyes with her fingers. She bucks her teeth.* PEACHES *is deeply disturbed. This should be the first strong indication that she's more psychoneurotic than simply a loveable eccentric.*)

COOKIE: I wish we had more kids than you an' Buddy. Another boy, maybe.

(*From off, we hear the ancient and frenzied bellow of* SHOOTER O'ROURKE.)

SHOOTER: (*Off*) Yooooohh, Cookie!!! Yooooohh, Peaches!!!

(COOKIE *nonchalantly crosses and opens the back door that the family always uses.* PEACHES *nonchalantly rises and opens the bathroom door [decorated with a painted quarter moon].* SHOOTER, *thickly bespectacled and with cane in hand, scurries in and makes a B-line for the bathroom, zinging one line in transit.*

SHOOTER: That gal arrive, yet???

PEACHES: No Gramps.

COOKIE: No, Daddy.

(COOKIE *closes the outside door,* PEACHES *the bathroom door. Both return to their costumes as though* SHOOTER's *entrance is a commonplace thing [which it is].*)

COOKIE: He made it.

PEACHES: He always makes it.

COOKIE: Almost always. (*Indicating a bucket and mop.*) We should stash the costumes before the girl gets here.

PEACHES: She's not a spy, Ma. She's a newscaster.

COOKIE: Right. Denise Walker. She's new. But arready she's my favorite. *(Collecting the costumes)* But we gotta be cagey...secretive. Lotsa other clubs would love to copy our costumes.

PEACHES: It's too late for the other clubs. The parade's this week.

COOKIE: That's why Brotherly Love wins so often. We prepare for next year soon as last year is over.

PEACHES: What about *this* year?

(COOKIE is stumped for a moment as GASPARI "HOAGIE" CATANIA enters. Grumpily, he takes off his expensive topcoat. He places it on an easy chair. PEACHES crosses and they kiss. He's dressed in a black suit and carries an attache' case. Throughout, PEACHES will apply his costume-in-progress to his body in order to check her work.)

PEACHES: Hiya Gas, whatsa matter? You look outta sorts.

GASPARI: Where's the geriatrics' Jesse Owens?

PEACHES: *(Thumbing towards the bathroom)* His clubhouse.

GASPARI: He needs a bladder bag. He knocked the groceries out of Mrs Levine's arms. Knocked the Ravinski kid offa her bike. I nearly got hit by a car getting out of his way.

COOKIE: *(Unconcerned)* You're insured.

GASPARI: Scared the hell out of me. Embarrassed me, too.

COOKIE: You shouldn't let a harmless little ole man scare you.

GASPARI: *"Harmless"*? We're talking about the Ho Chi Minh of Front Street. The Visigoth of Kensington.

COOKIE: You dress like that for work?

GASPARI: *(Almost preening)* Certainly. Any objections?

COOKIE: *(Shrugs)* You look like a gangster.

PEACHES: He shouldn't embarrass you. He's not *your* grandfather.

GASPARI: I'm embarrassed cause some people don't know that. He comes barreling down the street screaming, "Make way for a pissin' fool, Hoagie!"

COOKIE: So, he's got bad kidneys.

GASPARI: I'm a grown man and he still calls me that name.

COOKIE: We should be thankful for his energy.

GASPARI: Why can't he grow old gracefully?

PEACHES: Grace is *not* one of his attributes.

GASPARI: I've got a law degree. I'm a practicing attorney.

COOKIE: Quit practicin' and get it right.

GASPARI: An Ivy League graduate.

PEACHES: *(In weary anticipation)* Phi Beta Kappa.

GASPARI: I was getting to that.

COOKIE: Listen Gaspari, you keep gettin' worked up over Daddy's kidneys and he'll be at your funeral.

GASPARI: Probably urinate on my grave.

COOKIE: Y'know he's an independent operator. Always speaks what's on his mind.

GASPARI: If he spoke what's on his mind, he'd say nothing. It's bad enough he calls me that here. But when he goes screaming through the streets, his hand on his crotch yelling that stupid name -

SHOOTER: *(Emerging)* Hiya, Hoagie!!! Scared the shit outta ya, didn't I?

COOKIE: *(Shaking her finger)* Wash yer mouth out, Daddy.

GASPARI: If you can't make it home, then cut out the beer.

(SHOOTER looks at him as though GASPARI is insane.)

PEACHES: Gaspari...

GASPARI: I was just saying, "Why can't you grow old gracefully?"

SHOOTER: I can't get the hang of it.

PEACHES: Gas, turn it off.

COOKIE: Turn off the gas, Gas.

GASPARI: Keep outta this, Peaches.

SHOOTER: Hey, that's my granddaughter you're talkin' to.

GASPARI: It's my wife!

PEACHES: *(More or less to herself)* "It"?

SHOOTER: That only means you're *legally* related.

GASPARI: I know a thing or two about the law.

SHOOTER: Then you know you ain't blood. Ya can't get closer than blood.

GASPARI: *Miraculously,* Peaches transcends her genetics.

SHOOTER: You're a doctor too, huh?

(SHOOTER—using his cane—lifts GASPARI's coat from his favorite chair and drops it on the floor. GASPARI retrieves it and hands it to PEACHES who hangs it on a rack near the door.)

GASPARI: Your decline is truly pathetic, Shooter.

SHOOTER: You ain't seen nothin' yet.

GASPARI: You used to be the greatest heller in Kensington.

SHOOTER: Yeah, the goody-two-shoes said I'd pay in the end. They're all pushin' up daisies.

GASPARI: Have you ever reflected on the wasteful life you lived?

SHOOTER: *(Nodding)* Uh-huh.

GASPARI: Any regrets?

SHOOTER: My granddaughter coulda married better.
Listen, if I was doin' anythin' wrong—really wrong— He'd a taken me by now.

GASPARI: Maybe He doesn't want you.

SHOOTER: I apologize for out there. I'm arright when I'm sittin' an' havin' a beer an' tellin' stories to the boys. But when I leave the joint...well, my belly gets like...

PEACHES: Like a tempest in a teapot.

COOKIE: *(To PEACHES)* Hey, that's cute, honey. What's it mean?

GASPARI: *(Irritably to his wife)* Stop with the approbation! It's fuel to the fire.

SHOOTER: Clever girl, my Peaches. Ya don't appreciate. Don't appreciate none of us. *(Becoming maudlin)* Especially me.

COOKIE: See what ya done. Hoagie? *(Soothing him)* There, there Daddy. It's O K.

GASPARI: Strictly crocodile.

COOKIE: Stop the namecallin'. You...alligator!

GASPARI: Anything other than "Hoagie".

COOKIE: Don't cry, Daddy. Can we getcha a beer?

(He nods. PEACHES goes behind the bar.)

SHOOTER: I want Hoagie t'get it.

GASPARI: Not on your life.

SHOOTER: *(Morosely)* What little is left of it.

PEACHES: Gas...

COOKIE: *(To* GASPARI*)* Don't be so heartless.

GASPARI: *(Somewhat moved)* Well...perhaps. Only if you call me by my Christian name.

COOKIE: Bury the peacepipe, Daddy. Call Hoagie by his real name an' he'll getcha a cool one.

SHOOTER: If my name was Gaspari I'd beg t'be called Hoagie.

GASPARI: It has to do with heritage. It's Italian for Casper... One of the Magi that visited the baby Jesus.

SHOOTER: Was he the one that brung the pizza?

(He giggles until dart-like stares from the women cause SHOOTER *to apologize...)*

SHOOTER: A joke. Could I please have a little beer, Gas-par-ee?

*(*GASPARI *hesitates a moment, pops open a can and semi-taunts* SHOOTER *with the can.* SHOOTER *grabs at the elusive beer.)*

GASPARI: Now, that's more like it. It's not hard to be civil.

SHOOTER: No, it's not.

GASPARI: No harm done.

SHOOTER: You betcha.

GASPARI: Keeps peace in the family.

SHOOTER: The family is sacred.

GASPARI: *(Offering the beer, tentatively)* One for the family.

SHOOTER: Gaspari, words cannot express my gratitude.

GASPARI: That's more like it, Shooter. Now, beg. *(Waving the can at frustrated* SHOOTER*)* Like a dog.

COOKIE: No good will come of this, Ho-... Gaspari.

*(*GASPARI *finally relinquishes the can to the exasperated oldster.)*

GASPARI: Now, what do you say?

SHOOTER: Kiss my ass, Hoagie.

COOKIE: Gutter talk, Daddy.

GASPARI: Gutter talk. Rule of thumb in his saloon. So I hear.

SHOOTER: That reminds me. Spike's gonna be late tonight.

COOKIE: Of all nights.

SHOOTER: Kelly's on a toot, again. Spike gotta work overtime till Scanlon comes in. I gotta unload Kelly.

PEACHES: You always say that. He's been with ya for over twenty years. He goes onna bender every year when you give him his Christmas bonus.

SHOOTER: I oughtta give him his Christmas bonus in August when everyone's on vacation.

(TRIXIE *bounds in from outside.*)

TRIXIE: Yo, everybody.

PEACHES: Yo, Trix!

COOKIE: Yo, honey!

TRIXIE: Yo, Daddy! *(Kissing him)*

GASPARI: *(Brightening)* Yo, Trixie.

TRIXIE: Yo, Shooter. *(Kissing him)*

SHOOTER: Yo, honey.

TRIXIE: *(Hugging* COOKIE*)* Everythin' arright, Grandma?

COOKIE: Sure. Why wouldn't it be? New Year's Day comin' up. Y'know what that means?

TRIXIE: Uh...the tree comes down?

COOKIE: Stop yer joshin'. It's Mummers' day in Philly.

TRIXIE: *(Indicating the "mummerabilia")* How could I forget?

COOKIE: An' yer Uncle Buddy's gonna strut through that door.

(All *react uneasily to oblivious* COOKIE's *comment. After an awkward pause...*)

TRIXIE: Where's everyone else?

COOKIE: Yer grandpa's workin' overtime. Yer brother's shoppin' for finishin' touches for his costume.

(GASPARI *flinches at this.*)

TRIXIE: That jerk's takin' this parade a little too seriously.

GASPARI: That "jerk"'s your flesh and blood.

TRIXIE: I had no say in the matter.

COOKIE: He's not just a marcher no more. He's been promoted. "Fancy dress division".

TRIXIE: Skippy Riley says it's only 'cause he's Shooter's great grandson

COOKIE: Skippy's jealous cause he's still "clown division". The pits!

SHOOTER: I figured fancy dress for Franjo was...well, wish-fulfillment.

GASPARI: *(Darkly serious)* I want no innuendos when this girl arrives.

TRIXIE: My brother's not capable of innuendo.

GASPARI: *(A glare at* TRIXIE*)* Why are we assembling here tonight?

TRIXIE: I thought Shooter deserved a tribute. Being the oldest mummer.

SHOOTER: By all means.

COOKIE: I thought you didn't like our parade.

TRIXIE: I don't. I like Shooter.

GASPARI: It's awkward recording our attitudes...our idiosyncrasies on T V.

COOKIE: Whataya gotta hide?

GASPARI: For court, I prepare a brief. But I don't feel comfortable speaking extemporaneously.

SHOOTER: Then speak English like the rest of us.

(By now, PEACHES *has adorned* GASPARI *with a jabot and a replica of a military helmet with feathers and spangles.*

GASPARI: After all, I have an image to maintain.

PEACHES: Don't worry. *You* won't get much attention, tonight.

GASPARI: *(Somewhat hurt)* I won't?

TRIXIE: It's Shooter she's comin' to see.

SHOOTER: I still draw the dollies.

GASPARI: When is this... *(Deference to* TRIXIE*...)* ...newsperson due?

TRIXIE: A few minutes. And Franjo's due later.

GASPARI: *(Quietly)* The later the better.

TRIXIE: Time's irrelevant.

GASPARI: The hours you keep attest to that. You think your mother stayed out till all hours?

COOKIE: No, sirree! Midnight yer daddy hadda have her home... *(Soto voce)* but it didn't do any good.

GASPARI: *(Cutting off* COOKIE*)* What will she ask?

TRIXIE: She wants to know what it's like to be raised in a mummer family. I said it's like eating worms.

COOKIE: You usta *like* to eat worms. Can I say that on T V?

GASPARI: *(Indicating* COOKIE *to* TRIXIE*)* See what you've unleashed? How'd you get to be Dean's List?

TRIXIE: An' it ain't costin' you nothin', Daddy. Scholarship. Remember? *(Her finger to her temple)* Brains. In abundance.

GASPARI: *(Imitating)* "Ain't costin' you nothin'."
So, how come you talk like a gun moll?

TRIXIE: I'm a product of my environment.

GASPARI: *(Indicating the den)* Maybe this environment. Not my environment.

TRIXIE: Besides, my friends talk this way.

GASPARI: If your friends jumped off the Ben Franklin Bridge, would you?

TRIXIE: Sure, I'd rather be dead than lonely.

GASPARI: In my day you aspired to better yourself. You had respect for the values of the older generat— *(Spotting dozing* SHOOTER—*beer in hand— he sighs)*

PEACHES: *(Surreptitiously to* TRIXIE*)* Don't mention how your dad an' me, well...how we fight sometimes.

TRIXIE: The neighbors *know*, Ma. And you two only spat. Then it's kiss and make up. My friends parents' *fight*! They grew up in the trees.

COOKIE: Did you tell her how your great-grandfather embarrasses us?

TRIXIE: I told her he was an octogenarian lecher.

PEACHES: *(Indicating the dozing old man)* Only if they're under forty.

GASPARI: I may want to edit this tape. If I can't, I'll subpoena.

*(*SPIKE O'ROURKE *enters.* GASPARI *takes a* Wall Street Journal *from his case.)*

COOKIE: Yo, hon.

PEACHES: Yo, Pop.

TRIXIE: Yo, Gramps.

(She crosses and kisses him)

SPIKE: *(Wearily removing his coat with* COOKIE's *help)* Everybody goes crazy this time a'year.

SHOOTER: *(Awakening)* If it's too hot inna kitchen...open the window.

SPIKE: Enough, Daddy. I'm at the end of my rope. *(Kissing* COOKIE*)* What's for dinner?

COOKIE: Pepper pot. Your favorite.

SPIKE: Pepper pot, *again*? Every night this week... *(Getting a beer)*

COOKIE: Christmas in Philly. Pepper pot's traditional.

SPIKE: T'hell with tradition. How d'ya think people in Denver... Atlanta get along without pepper pot?

COOKIE: But they don't hafta march six miles on New Year's Day. Pepper pot's a pepper-upper. It says so on the label.

SPIKE: *Canned* pepper pot??? Since when?

COOKIE: *(Defensively)* I been busy, Spike. An' only the stew's canned. Not the tripe!

TRIXIE: Tripe! *(Faux-gagging)* Grandma's delicacy is another's bait.

SPIKE: When is this broad gonna be here?

TRIXIE: *Woman*, Grandpa. She's in my women's group.

SPIKE: *(Winking to his father)* The last girlfriend you brought around was nothin' but broad. *(He gestures a weighty pair of hips to his father)* Huh, Daddy?

(SHOOTER—and the others—ignore him. Unappreciated, he continues to TRIXIE...)

SPIKE: Where's yer brother?

TRIXIE: Shopping for his costume.

SPIKE: *(Shaking his head in dismay)* Maybe we can do this interview before he gets here. Beer, Hoagie?

(A grim shake of the head from GASPARI. SPIKE continues...)

SPIKE: Too good t'drink with us, huh? *(To his wife and daughter)* How's the work comin', girls?

COOKIE: You're gonna be real proud of us, Spike.

PEACHES: You guys are gonna look handsome on the first.

SHOOTER: Gimmee a beer, Spike.

SPIKE: *(Going behind the bar)* Sure, Daddy.

SHOOTER: Make it two. Save ya a trip.

SPIKE: *(To TRIXIE)* Don't it bother you, yer mother an' grandma workin' their fingers t'the bone for Brotherly Love? You sit twiddlin' yer thumbs?

TRIXIE: It bothers me more than a bit.

SPIKE: Well, give 'em a hand. This is a community effort.

TRIXIE: It ain't my community.

SPIKE: Peaches... Hoagie... where'd you go wrong with this one? *(Aside to his father)* T'say nothin' of Franjo.

GASPARI: She'd rather improve her mind than her sewing.

COOKIE: You can do both. Brains aren't enough.

(The front door rings. Trixie starts to ascend to answer.

TRIXIE: I'll get it. If sewin was fun, men would be doin' it. *(She ascends the stairs.)*

(Despite their objections, SHOOTER and SPIKE seem genuinely proud of her.)

SHOOTER: Feisty little brat, ain't she?

SPIKE: So why does she talk like those bimboes that hang offa my bar?

SHOOTER: *MY* bar, sonny. I ain't dead yet.

SPIKE: Course not, Daddy. *(Beat)* An' even the bimboes're loyal mummerettes. Never miss a party an' never miss a parade.

GASPARI: Naturally. It's a free drunk.

SPIKE: A cheap drunk. Nothin's free!
Peaches, don't her talk upset you?

PEACHES: Daddy, nothin' about my family upsets me anymore.

SHOOTER: Right, honey. Let others do the worryin'. You'll live longer.

PEACHES: Anyway, she's heard worse around here.

SPIKE: Only in times of crises.

GASPARI: Like when you run out of beer.

SPIKE/SHOOTER: We *never* run outta beer.

SPIKE: Hey, maybe we should stash the costumes from the T V.

GASPARI: God, are you paranoid.

SPIKE: Paranoid! That's what they called Butch O'Malley when he welshed on that bet with Scarfazio. Ya seen what happened t'Butch.

COOKIE: He got hit by a car, Spike. He didn't get rubbed out.

SPIKE: The accident was a rub-out.

COOKIE: G'wan, the driver was eighty-three an' half-blind.

SPIKE: Her name was Donatello. They all stick together.

(GASPARI shakes his head in despair as SPIKE continues...)

SPIKE: People told Butch that he was paranoid so he started believin' them...started lookin' over his shoulder alla time. One day he stepped offa curb lookin' over his shoulder an' splat!

COOKIE: That's all she wrote for Butch.

GASPARI: *(Quietly, in disbelief)* Jesus Christ.

SPIKE: Scarfazio couldn'a planned it better. I betcha he started the paranoid talk. *(To* GASPARI*)* An' don't go takin' God's name in vain. This is a religious, Church-goin' household.

COOKIE: I go every mornin'. Pray for the family.

GASPARI: There aren't enough days in the week for that, Cookie.

COOKIE: Daddy's goin' back again lately.

SHOOTER: I'm crammin' fer my finals.

SPIKE: Now girls, put the costumes inna back room.

GASPARI: *(Militantly to his wife)* You obey him and I leave this room forever.

SPIKE: Obey your father, honey. Kill two birds with one stone.

GASPARI: Peaches, I'm warning you...

PEACHES: Will you two cut it out? We're expectin' a guest.

SHOOTER: Leave 'em alone! It's gettin' good.

SPIKE: *(To* GASPARI, *intensifying)* Are you givin' orders in *my* house?

SHOOTER: It's *my* house, jerkeroo!

SPIKE: In my father's house, you're givin' orders to my daughter???

*(*TRIXIE, DENISE *and a T V cameraman [*BARRY*] start to descend unnoticed as the action heats up. He carries a camera labeled "W C A U—Channel 10".)*

SHOOTER: It's my granddaughter!!!

GASPARI: IT'S MY WIFE!!!

PEACHES: IT??? WHO'S AN "IT"? I'M A HUMAN BEING!!!

*(*SHOOTER *pops up and energetically starts moving furniture as he shouts...)*

SHOOTER: GIVE 'EM ROOM!!! GET THE GLOVES, COOKIE!!!

COOKIE: *(As calm as the others are excited)* Let 'em talk it out. Cool heads will prevail.

SPIKE: *(Nose to nose with* GASPARI*)* Ya think yer talkin' t'some bum inna park???

GASPARI: I'd *rather* be talking to some bum in the park!!!

SPIKE: *(Rolling up his sleeves)* I gotta good mind to—

GASPARI: *You've* got a good mind??? If they put your brain in a worm's head it would crawl backwards!!!

SHOOTER: *(Suddenly breaking for the bathroom)* Yooooooohhhhh!!!

(He makes his destination and the attention shifts.)

PEACHES: Oh hiya, Trix. We...uh, thought you were still upstairs.

TRIXIE: We can go back up. Then the family beast can roar.

GASPARI: *(Subdued and diplomatic)* Spike and I were just discussing the interview.

(SPIKE is thrown a bit between the altercation and the realization that there's a black guest in the house. He should never be offensive...just confused by the world's changes [as usual].)

SPIKE: That's right, Hoa—...uh, Gaspari.

TRIXIE: Take a walk, you two. Cool off. While Denise conducts the interview.

SHOOTER: Good idea, Trixie. We don't need them two, anyway.

COOKIE: Innerductions are in order, Trix. *(To DENISE)* I mean, we don't need no innerduction t'you, Miss Walker. You talk to us every night.

TRIXIE: My grandmother talks back, Denise.

DENISE: *(Graciously to COOKIE)* How sweet of you.

COOKIE: I'm glad for your opportunity. I left Belfast as a girl causa prejudice. But there it wasn't color. It was rel-

(As often happens, COOKIE has become an embarrassment with a forthright statement. The family is semi-mortified but DENISE is oddly intrigued while TRIXIE steers her away.)

TRIXIE: I'll start with the youngest and work my way up. Actually, Franjo's at the bottom.

SPIKE: *(Jovially)* You can say that, again.

(GASPARI elbows him in the ribs.)

TRIXIE: But he's not here. Then there's me.

DENISE: "Trixie"?

TRIXIE: *(Slightly embarrassed)* Grandma's name.

COOKIE: Angela's her real name. Angela Catania. *(With her unconscious disdain)* Sounds "right offa the boat".

GASPARI: After my mother.

TRIXIE: Grandma's into dog names.

COOKIE: Not dog names. Cute names.

TRIXIE: Cute when you're in the crib. Not when you're nineteen years-old. She's got a sister she calls "Skipper".

PEACHES: Trix! She's pullin' yer leg, Miss Walker.

DENISE: Call me Denise.

COOKIE: Oh, I always do. Every night at six. "Let's watch De—

GASPARI: Honey, the introductions. It's getting late and I've got to close a deal in the morning.

SPIKE: Pay your loan shark?

(Everyone laughs lightly, GASPARI less than the others.)

TRIXIE: This is my dad.

DENISE: Pleased I'm sure.

GASPARI: *(Extending his hand)* Gaspari Catania. "Bernstein, Catania, Ryan, Ortiz and Shabbaz". *(Innocently patronizing)* In fact, Shabbaz is our—

DENISE: *(Shaking pleasantly)* Yeah, I kind of figured.

TRIXIE: And my mom.

PEACHES: Pleased.

DENISE: Same here. Angela's a sweetie.

TRIXIE: And my grandfather, Spike.

SPIKE: *(Awkwardly attempting to shake)* How ya doin'?

DENISE: *(Shaking his hand)* Hi, Spike.

SPIKE: I never know... y'know, whether to shake hands with a lady.

TRIXIE: And finally... *(Looking to the bathroom)* What's he doing?

COOKIE: I don't hear no groanin'. It must be—

SHOOTER: *(Emerging)* Emptied out the ole teapot.

DENISE: You must be the famous Shooter O'Rourke I've heard so much about.

SHOOTER: *(Extending his hand)* Don't worry. I washed.

(She extends her hand, they shake. SHOOTER pulls her towards him and the family awkwardly intervenes with reactions that run from embarrassment to amusement. DENISE is a bit unnerved.)

COOKIE: *(Apologetically to DENISE)* It's the excitement.

SHOOTER: Excitement? Around here? With you deadbeats? Don't make me laugh. *(Beat)* Give the girl a drink. *(To BARRY)* The fella, too.

DENISE: Barry, my cameraman, folks.

(Greetings all around and DENISE continues...)

DENISE: Skip the drink. I'm on the job.

SHOOTER: So? My help drinks on the job. Whataya do, honey?

GASPARI: She's here to interview you. Remember?

SHOOTER: Oh, yeah. I thought I recognized you from here. *(Pointing to the T V set)* Down at the bar we watch Channel 3. But she's getting' fat. Spike, from now on we watch this girl.

(SPIKE nods obediently.)

DENISE: Thanks. T V tends to make you look heavier...flattten you out.

SHOOTER: Nothin' flat on your chassis.

TRIXIE: O K, Shooter. Cut the macho.

SHOOTER: "Macho"? What's "macho"? You teachin' her Eye-talian, Hoagie?

DENISE: *(Almost at a loss)* My, you mummers are...a high-spirited bunch.

(TRIXIE fakes a finger down her throat and gags. The others are irritated. DENISE is disconcerted. BARRY smiles as he continues setting up his equipment.)

SPIKE: You sabotage us, Trix, you'll be sabotagin' Miss Walker as well.

COOKIE: You can't give birth to a little mummer with an attitude like that.

TRIXIE: Marriage is a trap conceived by men for free labor.

COOKIE: How're you gonna have kids, then?

TRIXIE: If I so choose, Grandma, there are ways.

(COOKIE looks to PEACHES who looks away as TRIXIE continues...)

TRIXIE: I'd break my baby's legs before I'd let him march.

COOKIE: Ever since that *Exorcist* movie, I'm tellin' ya...

TRIXIE: *(Demonically miming)* Snap! Snap!

GASPARI: Cut that talk, young lady.

PEACHES: She's showin' off, Gas.

SHOOTER: *(To DENISE, indicating TRIXIE)* She's cute, ain't she?

TRIXIE: *(Kissing SHOOTER on the cheek)* Thanks, Shooter.

PEACHES: *(To SHOOTER)* You spoiled 'er. She's gettin' t'be more like you every day.

SHOOTER: *(Beaming)* Yeah, I know.

DENISE: *(Looking to BARRY)* I think we're ready, Angela.

SHOOTER: *(Befuddled)* Angela? Who's Angela?

DENISE: Please be patient. I'm new in town but I've researched the parade.

SHOOTER: That won't work. You gotta be there.

DENISE: I'm sure. I'll approach the subject from the mummers' mystique.

COOKIE: The what???

TRIXIE: Clam up, Grandma. Let's get this over with.

GASPARI: None of that smart-mouthed disrespect on the air.

DENISE: It can be erased.

TRIXIE: We can all be erased with the push of a button.

COOKIE: Ain't technology grand?

DENISE: Everyone relaxed?

SHOOTER: I'm relaxed.

(He crosses to DENISE)

DENISE: *(Taking the mike and addressing SHOOTER)* Say what you feel.

(The camera lights go on. SHOOTER surreptitiously grabs DENISE by the rear as he says...)

SHOOTER: Nice ass!

(Pandemonium! DENISE is shaken. BARRY turns off the power. The others are humiliated and separate SHOOTER from the newscaster. TRIXIE is especially angry.)

TRIXIE: COME ON, DENISE! You don't deserve this.

(She starts to lead DENISE up the stairs.)

SHOOTER: Hey Trix, I thought you were on *my* side.

DENISE: *(Composing herself)* No, no, Trixie. We'll just edit that out. I asked for it.

SHOOTER: An' I gave it to ya.

TRIXIE: *(In his face)* You think bein' old allows you to do that???

SHOOTER: It makes it easier.

DENISE: *(Taking TRIXIE aside)* Would he have done that to a *white* woman?

TRIXIE: *(A surprised beat)* Of course. If she was as attractive as you.

DENISE: *(Reconsidering her irritation)* Oh. In that case...

SHOOTER: I didn't mean it, Trix.

TRIXIE: Don't apologize to me.

SHOOTER: I'm sorry, Miss Walker.

DENISE: Let's pretend it didn't happen.

SHOOTER: It didn't happen.

DENISE: Shall we begin?

(SHOOTER *closes in on her but he's held at bay, primarily by* PEACHES.)

DENISE: Well, here we are in late December just three days short of America's bi-centennial. And for most of these 200 years Philadelphia's mummers have marched on New Year's Day.

SPIKE: *(Interjecting)* A hundred and fourteen years.

DENISE: Today we view the pageant through the eyes of the only family in history with four generations marching simultaneously.

COOKIE: All at the same time, too.

DENISE: *(Nodding to* COOKIE*)* So we turn to the living embodiment of mummer's history, the venerable "Mummer of Them All", Mister Francis "Shooter" O'Rourke.

(DENISE *will shift the mike from speaker to speaker [keeping a safe distance from* SHOOTER*]. The interview format will soon give way to a forum, often heated.*)

SHOOTER: *(Smiling at the camera)* That's me. I'm Shooter.

DENISE: How old were you when you first marched?

SPIKE: He was four–

SHOOTER: Shut up, Motormouth! This is my show. You weren't even alive when I first marched. None of ya were. If it weren't for me none of ya would be on this here T V. Get that straight!

DENISE: *(Nervously interjecting)* My. Four years of age. Can you remember it?

SHOOTER: Like it was yesterday.

DENISE: Really?

SHOOTER: No, not really! Who d'ya think I am, God?

DENISE: Hardly. I suppose you've seen a lot of changes?

SHOOTER: Certainly I've seen changes. What the hell kinda question–

DENISE: *(Interjecting)* What's the most significant change, Mister O'Rourke?

SHOOTER: That's a change. People used to call me Shooter, not Mister. Like I got one foot in the grave. Another change...these new mummers have made the parade a crock a'—

(TRIXIE *squeezes his arm. He grimaces.*)

SHOOTER: *(Smarting from her pressure)* Leggo, ya little bitch.

GASPARI: Could we delete the expletives?

BARRY: No problem.

SHOOTER: The new mummers lack tradition.

(He looks to GASPARI *who nods agreeably.)*

DENISE: Could you expand on that?

SHOOTER: Sure, they're a bunch of piss-ants...candy-asses...

(A chorus of sighs)

DENISE: I mean, could you elaborate upon the issues?

SHOOTER: Sure, honey. We usta ride horses an' carry guns. We'd put on make-up an' costumes we made ourselves...not let the wives do it. We'd shoot an' yell till they'd put booze an' food on the doorstep then. If we was satisfied, we'd recite a poem. Nothin' sissy, y'know. A man's poem. An' nothin' phoney. It rhymed. *(He belts one out with gusto)*
Here we stand at your front door
Just as we did the year before.
Open the door an' let us in,
Give us all a drink a'gin.
Or better, give us somethin' hot,
A steamin' bowl of pepper pot.
Hey Trix, who was that poet you was studyin' last week?

TRIXIE: T S Eliot.

SHOOTER: Never heard of him.

TRIXIE: *(Dryly)* Surprise.

SHOOTER: What'd he write?

TRIXIE: *The Wasteland.*

SHOOTER: Bet that's a lotta laughs. Could he write a poem like I just said?

TRIXIE: Not in a million years.

SHOOTER: *(Back to* DENISE*)* Then we'd do the Mummer's Strut. Not this two-step they do today. An' alla the people would cheer an' march with us down Broad Street.

DENISE: Did anyone ever get shot?

SHOOTER: We'd all be juiced up but we'd stagger along.

DENISE: I mean the gunplay.

SHOOTER: Once in a while. But the tough ones kept marchin'. Trix, my pistol.

*(*TRIXIE *crosses and fetches the pistol.)*

COOKIE: Daddy's the only one allowed to carry a pistol, nowadays.

PEACHES: Honorary, y'know. No bullets, just blanks.

SHOOTER: That's the toughest thing about agein'. Shootin' blanks.

GASPARI: Why don't you tell-

SHOOTER: Shut up, Hoagie. I got the floor.

DENISE: Hoagie???

PEACHES: A high school nickname.

GASPARI: As you may know Denise, there are three divisions in the parade.

SHOOTER: There's the clowns. The bottom of the barrel. The boobs with no talent 'cept to fall down. *(Indicating SPIKE)* My son, here...he was a clown for forty-six years.

SPIKE: I happened to like bein' a clown.

GASPARI: Came natural to you, Spike.

SHOOTER: Four years ago, he tried a cartwheel. Imagine! A man his age. *(To SPIKE)* You wouldn'a made it even if you were sober.

SPIKE: I wouldn'a *tried* it if I was sober. *(Bitterly to GASPARI)* Thought that was funny, didn't ya?

GASPARI: It was only funny to watch.

PEACHES: Hey Gas, a little compassion, huh?

COOKIE: A blessin' in disguise. Spike got promoted to string band division.

DENISE: What instrument?

SPIKE: *(Hesitantly)* Well, uh...bass drum.

TRIXIE: He carries it.

GASPARI: And then there's the elite division. Fancy dress. That's me.

COOKIE: And Daddy's head of the whole shebang.

DENISE: Angela showed me last year's pictures. Before the riot. *(To SHOOTER)* You looked very impressive.

SHOOTER: I wear my old-timey outfit cause I'm a legend. That all changed with Captain Tom Daly back in 1921. He led Billy Penn Mummers Club. Wore a costume sixty feet long, Needed a hundred and thirty guys to carry it.

DENISE: Ostentatious.

SHOOTER: Yeah that's goin' overboard. Ever since Daly, it's been costumes over fun. They been more an' more...well, f'rinstance...two years ago, that sissy freedom outfit wanted t'march.

TRIXIE: *(Militantly)* Gay Liberation, Shooter!

GASPARI/SPIKE: *(Simultaneously)* Do we have to listen to this?This definitely gotta be erased.

SHOOTER: *(Ignoring them)* The Mummers nearly went crazy 'til I got onna bullhorn an' says, "What's the big deal? The mummers got twenty thousand peacocks struttin' around in silks an' satins an' feathers." That shut 'em up. So the parade allowed the homos. Only they passed. No fuss was bein' made so they went home angry.

SPIKE: But still gay. Y'know Daddy, if anyone else had talked to the mummers that way... a knuckle sandwich.

SHOOTER: Like the whippin' *you* got last year, huh?

SPIKE: Bite yer tongue about last year, Daddy. *(Aside to DENISE)* This gotta go.

TRIXIE: Shooter's right about last year. Brotherly Love's a paper tiger. They talk big when they're at Shooter's drinkin' shots an' beers.

GASPARI: Just for the record, I don't go to Shooter's.

DENISE: Let's talk about this year. I undersand that each club has a different theme and each operates under the strictest secrecy.

SPIKE: The Pentagon could learn from us.

DENISE: I don't suppose I could have a little hint...off the record.

SPIKE: Outta the question.

GASPARI: "A Tribute to The American Military"

SPIKE: *(Appalled)* DAMMIT, HOAGIE!!! YOU DUMB GUINEA!!!

PEACHES: POP, STOP CALLIN' GASPARI NAMES!!!

TRIXIE: I'M HALF-ITALIAN, GRANDPA!!!

SPIKE: Not the *better* half, honey. Accident of birth.

COOKIE: *(Aside to PEACHES)* "Accident" is right.

(PEACHES subdues her.)

GASPARI: Why get excited? Trixie probably tipped her off.

TRIXIE: Certainly I tipped 'er off.

DENISE: *(Flustered)* Well, I wanted to hear it firsthand.

TRIXIE: I'm firsthand. Saturated with mummery since I was in the cradle.

DENISE: Why a tribute to the American military?

COOKIE: It's a perfect choice what with Buddy comin ho-

(Before DENISE *can expand on* COOKIE's *comment, the others band together to "cover". They practically overlap one another.)*

PEACHES: A natural for Philly. Cradle of liberty.

SPIKE: Declaration of Independence.

GASPARI: Ben Franklin.

PEACHES: Valley Forge.

TRIXIE: The vast majority of colonists were anti-war.

GASPARI: Trixie, you're being taught by some of those sixties radicals. Now they have soft jobs. Fat salaries. Homes in the suburbs. *(To* DENISE*)* We wanted a patriotic theme. Good for the economy. The American flag attracts the consumer like the red flag attracts the bull.

DENISE: *(Becoming more assertive)* What about, "A penny saved is a penny earned"?

GASPARI: I would caution you to refrain from debate. Aside from being treasurer of the Bar Association, I've been a member of—

TRIXIE: She knows, Daddy. I gave her your resume. Like you told me.

GASPARI: Franklin was speaking figuratively in his almanac. If everyone saved, the country would go bankrupt.

SPIKE: Speakin' of pennies...can I put in two of mine? We're tryna talk to today's youth. *(Snidely towards* TRIXIE*)* The ones that still listen. Some of 'em won't look for jobs.

TRIXIE: What jobs?

SPIKE: Some, I said. Not all of 'em live offa welfare...steal. They're not all drugheads...longhairs.

TRIXIE: The Continental Army had long hair.

SPIKE: Maybe there weren't any barbers.

TRIXIE: Booze is a drug.

SPIKE: I think you're a drug, Trix. Everytime you mouth off I get an overdose. You've never seen me hallucinate.

TRIXIE: I've seen you pass out.

DENISE: *(Getting to her point)* Why are *women* excluded from the parade?

(Pause all around as TRIXIE *smugly nods.)*

GASPARI: Not true...technically.

COOKIE: We make the costumes.

DENISE: Why don't you march?

COOKIE: *(Shrugs)* We don't have no costumes.

PEACHES: It's tradition.

COOKIE: It'd be turmoil. There's enough turmoil in the world.

PEACHES: Besides, there's a Miss Mummers every year.

SPIKE: Yeah, that Polock kid last year.

SHOOTER: All tits an' ass.

DENISE: Wasn't the Declaration of Independence for all the people?

TRIXIE: Only half of them.

SPIKE: Sure it was. But where was Betsy Ross?

COOKIE: At Fourth and Carpenter where the D Bus stops.

SPIKE: Home sewin' for the boys onna battlefield. Just like today.

SHOOTER: We had girls, years ago.

SPIKE: Onna sly, ya did. *(To* DENISE*)* They snuck 'em in onna Q T. They'd be dressed like the guys.

GASPARI: That was a clear violation of the rules, Shooter.

COOKIE: They weren't what you'd call "good girls".

SHOOTER: We didn't want "good girls". We wanted fun. So did the girls.

DENISE: *(Pointedly)* And what about blacks?

(An awkward pause all around. Finally...)

GASPARI: They're allowed to apply. It's in the statutes.

TRIXIE: I wouldn't worry about it, Denise. What self-respecting black would want to mar-

SPIKE: We accepted that club a few years back. But they never showed up.

TRIXIE: That was the year you quadrupled the initiation fees.

GASPARI: Inflation.

SPIKE: *(Self-righteously to* DENISE*)* We stopped wearin' blackface.

TRIXIE: Court order.

COOKIE: We meant no harm. People should be able to laugh at themselves.

SPIKE: We march past their neighborhoods with free entertainment, candy for the kids. They just stare out their windows, lookin' grim.

COOKIE: I guess mummery ain't in their blood.

SHOOTER: We had darkies.

(Oblivious to DENISE's *wide-eyed reaction)*

SHOOTER: Octavius V. Cato Club back in '29 was the last.

COOKIE: Not darkies, Daddy. Colored.

GASPARI: Negro, Cookie.

TRIXIE: Black, Daddy.

SPIKE: Depression did 'em in. Did lots of clubs in.

SHOOTER: That was part of it. But they really wanted out. Couldn't blame 'em. They couldn't come t'the victory party in '29. I fought that. I said, "Fer Chrissakes, how can you keep 'em out? They was the best club in the parade!"

GASPARI: You're not an objective reporter, Miss Walker. Hardly on our side.

DENISE: I'm not aware that sides were chosen.

GASPARI: You seem to have little respect for our organization.

*(*SHOOTER *is dozing off in an easy chair.)*

TRIXIE: *(Trying to diplomatically intervene)* Hey, hey, why don't we show Denise the Mummer's Strut?

GASPARI: *(Badgering* DENISE*)* It may seem ludicrous that a man of my accomplishments should engage in such frivolity. But it's like Church... Family... Country. I don't appreciate strangers knocking it.

SPIKE: Atta boy, Ho—... Atta boy, Gaspari.

DENISE: Well, I'm sorry I gave that impression.

TRIXIE: *(Nervously)* C'mon, how 'bout the costumes?

SPIKE: *(Panicky)* No costumes!!! They ain't ready.

COOKIE: Almost ready. Finishin' touches is all.

SPIKE: *(Pondering)* No T V?

DENISE: No T V. Barry...

*(*BARRY—*who has lit up a cigarette—turns the camera off. A flourish of activity.* COOKIE *and* PEACHES *head for the back room.* SHOOTER *pops awake.)*

TRIXIE: *(To* BARRY *as she crosses to the record player)* No smoking in here, Barry.

(The women emerge with costumes, including a huge, plumed backpiece.)

SHOOTER: It's New Years, arready?

GASPARI: We're just going to show the girl, here.

SHOOTER: I'll get my old one. I ain't put on five pounds in fifty years.

(He heads for the glass-enclosed case to put on the shabby, dusty tramp's outfit, including spats, floppy shoes, baggy pants and a bright red vest. He strips to his long johns but—in a rare display of modesty—he scurries behind the bar to dress. The women help the men dress over their streetwear.)

BARRY: *(To* TRIXIE *though he's yet to put out the smoke)* Hey, whattaya say we meet for a beer later?

TRIXIE: How about one now, Barry?

BARRY: *(Seeing that* DENISE *is distracted)* Onna Q.T. *(*TRIXIE *grabs a beer and surreptitiously shakes it. Crossing to* BARRY, *she opens the can in his face thus extinguishing his cigarette [and his ardor].)*

*(*GASPARI's *costume is a bizarre potpourri of war-related objects i.e. outsized medals, a red, white and blue soldier's garb [including helmet], a papier-maché rifle and accoutrements like tiny tanks or airplanes. He also wears a cape with the stars and stripes.* SPIKE's *costume - on the other hand - is limited by the fact that it was made by* COOKIE. *It's an ill-fitting Civil War [Union] uniform that isn't nearly finished and isn't greatly exaggerated from the original Of course, they gab over the dressing.)*

DENISE: Would someone care to comment on last year's troubles?

SPIKE: We won first place. That aint trouble.

TRIXIE: Denise means with New Quakers Mummers Club.

SHOOTER: Those sons-a-bitches!

SPIKE: We lost the battle but we won the war.

SHOOTER: We won the battle, too.

COOKIE: Didja tell Denise the details, Trix?

TRIXIE: I tried to but I was laughin' too hard.

SPIKE: A lotta respect we get from your kids, Hoagie.

COOKIE: Say, where's Franjo?

SPIKE: Let the sleepin' dog lie.

DENISE: What's your version of the altercation, Shooter?

SHOOTER: Huh?

TRIXIE: The brawl between Brotherly Love and New Quakers.

SHOOTER: *(Perplexed)* When?

TRIXIE: Last year!

SHOOTER: Wuzzat last year?

SPIKE: Y'see, every year New Quakers finishes second t'Brotherly Love. Furthermore, we are from Kensington and we go down t'South Philly an' kick their butts in their own backyard. See, the Quakers came as "King Arthur And His Knights".

COOKIE: "Bad cess", says I, soon as I seen the weapons.

SPIKE: We came as "The Scottish Highlanders". Well, we outstrutted, an' outplayed, an' outclowned 'em. So—like always—we win first prize. The Quakers finish second... like kissin' yer sister.

COOKIE: We stop in this South Philly joint for a victory drink.

DENISE: Uh-oh!

COOKIE: This year, come home t' Kensington t' celebrate.

SPIKE: In pops "King Arthur and His Knights".

COOKIE: Like they was in search of The Holy Grail. Or a fight.

SPIKE: They starts in razzin' us.

COOKIE: Cause they wore dresses.

SPIKE: *Kilts,* not dresses! They'd say silly stuff like, "Ya wear pantyhouse under them skirts, girls?" We'd laugh. Only things started gettin' ugly. They'd lift up our kilts with their swords.
Suddenly a bottle fulla booze lands in the middle of the Quakers.

GASPARI: Witnesses said Shooter threw it.

SHOOTER: I'd'a never throwed a full bottle.

SPIKE: An we gotta battle guys wearin' armor.

GASPARI: To say nothing of their swords.

COOKIE: Not real. But sharp. You shoulda seen Spike's behind.

(General laughter)

DENISE: My word, how did it end?

SPIKE: Cops came. Bloody noses. Black eyes. Teeth. The usual.

SHOOTER: The biggest injury was the bass drum over Spike's head.

DENISE: *(To SPIKE)* What happened to you?

SHOOTER: To him, nothin'. But the drum was ruined.

DENISE: Did you part amicably?

SPIKE: Huh?

SHOOTER: *(Going for the gun)* Hell, no!!! Why I might just load this thing with the real McCoy on the first.

COOKIE: *(Adamantly)* Well, perish that thought!

PEACHES: He's kiddin', Ma. C'mon guys, strut yer stuff for Denise.

GASPARI: Ready, Trix?

PEACHES: *(To* TRIXIE*)* What're you playin'?

TRIXIE: "Golden Slippers". What else?

*(*TRIXIE *switches on the phonograph as* PEACHES *helps* GASPARI *with the magnificent backpiece. Despite his earlier "ego-defensiveness" about his involvement as a mummer,* GASPARI *beams.)*

COOKIE: *(To* DENISE*)* Hold onta yer hat, honey.

(The string band version of Oh Dem Golden Slippers *sets the three men off doing the "Mummer's strut".* COOKIE *and* PEACHES *clap and stomp but never join in. Shooter will fire an occasional blank.* DENISE *is genuinely fascinated by the sight [if not engaged] and even* TRIXIE *is surprisingly involved. The marcher's arms are extended horizontally and the body is bent at the waist as the knees kick high. The "strutters" go back, forth and to the sides and in circles as the spirit moves them.)*

(Suddenly, the outside door flies open and FRANJO *bursts in. He wears a replica of his father's cape. But he also wears red, white and blue make-up. He joins in with the other Mummers.)*

(At first, he goes unnoticed. Eventually, SHOOTER *notices and they lock arms and strut.* GASPARI *takes notice and reacts heartily for a moment or two. Then the reality of* FRANJO *sinks in and...*

FRANJO: HAPPY NEW YEAR, YOU MUMMA MOTHAS!!!

(Feverishly, GASPARI *grabs a bar towel and rushes across the room to wipe the make-up from his son's face.* SHOOTER—*with a "Yoooohhhh"—heads for the john. In general, all hell breaks loose.)*

GASPARI: *(Outraged)* YOU'VE BEEN WALKING THE STREETS IN MAKE-UP AGAIN???

FRANJO: *(Sounding like a street kid in spite of his image)* So what? Why do I have to wait for the first?

GASPARI: Because it's a law.

FRANJO: It's not a *law*!

GASPARI: O K, it's a rule.

*(*GASPARI *heatedly removes his costume as* PEACHES *helps with his backpiece.)*

FRANJO: Some lawyer! So, you think the American military plays by the rules?

SPIKE: *(Cynically to his grandson)* You'll get a deferment.

FRANJO: *(To his father)* Rules were made to be broken.

GASPARI: You sound like your sister!

SPIKE: With that hair an' make-up, he *more than sounds* like his sis—

GASPARI: *(To SPIKE)* You shut up!!!

SPIKE: Who're you tellin' t'shut up???

PEACHES: *(Heavenward)* Lord, all I ask is one week of the year in peace.

GASPARI: It's not one week. It's affecting his whole life. It's affecting my whole life.

COOKIE: There ya go, thinkin' on yerself again, Hoagie.

GASPARI: I don't know why I have to take this.

COOKIE: You take it 'cause you love Peaches.

GASPARI: But I wamt to divorce my in-laws.

COOKIE: Don't talk divorce. Divorce means excommunication.

GASPARI: *(To PEACHES)* We're going home.

DENISE: *(Quietly)* Could I have a word with you, Franjo?

GASPARI: No you can't.

FRANJO: Who's she?

GASPARI: *(Preparing to leave)* Trixie, come on.

TRIXIE: What about Denise?

GASPARI: T'hell with Denise.

DENISE: *(To DENISE)* I'll be alright.

GASPARI: One word about my son on T V, I'll have you up on libel charges.

DENISE: I'm protected by the First Amendment.

GASPARI: T'hell with The First Amendment.

DENISE: Franjo, I'm always looking for a story. If you'd like some T V access about your obsession-

FRANJO: Obsession? My family thinks it's an affliction.

SPIKE: Deviation!!!

DENISE: Nevertheless, if you'd like a public forum...

FRANJO: They're not pissed enough at me? I should go public???

GASPARI: *(To DENISE)* I'll talk to you in the morning.

(Neglecting to remove his helmet, GASPARI *herds his family out the door, slamming it behind. A long, nervous silence)*

COOKIE: *(Finally, to* DENISE*)* That was Franjo.

SPIKE: Sure was.

COOKIE: He's gettin' in shape for the parade.

(The phone rings.)

SHOOTER: *(Off) (From the bathroom)* DON'T NOBODY TOUCH THAT!!! *(He bounds out of the bathroom, and B-lines it to the phone. Speaking surreptitiously...)* Shooter, here.

(His conversation will be brief - and under the other dialogue - consisting of "yeah"s, "gotcha"s and "you betcha"s.)

DENISE: Well Barry, I guess we got what we came for.

BARRY: More! I'm gonna split with the truck.

DENISE: Yes, I'll talk to you in the morning.

BARRY: Not before the lawyer guy talks to you, I bet. *(To* SPIKE *and* COOKIE*)* So long, folks. It was... uh,...bizarre. *(Exits)*

COOKIE: *(Goofily to* DENISE*)* That's the mummers. One big bazaar.

SHOOTER: *(Hanging up and crossing to* DENISE*)* What about you, Toots? You need a ride?

DENISE: I came in my own car. Around the corner.

SPIKE: I'll walk ya. Yer a stranger in these parts.

DENISE: Decidedly.

SHOOTER: Take a powder. She's innerested in me. Beside, you're married.

SPIKE: *(Shaking his head)* Daddy, if Momma was alive...

SHOOTER: Momma's been dead for twenty-six years. Grow up. Get over it. *(To* DENISE*)* Hey honey, gimmee a chance to change.

(He goes back behind the bar to change with all due respect. COOKIE *helps* SPIKE *remove his costume over his streetwear.)*

COOKIE: Who phoned, Daddy?

SHOOTER: Stinky Flaherty.

COOKIE: Why're you associatin' with the likes a'him?

SHOOTER: Uh... he, uh... He owes me some dough. He's down at the joint. I better take the gun. Stinky's a rough customer.

DENISE: *(Nervously)* Perhaps I'd be safer on my own.

COOKIE: Not around here, dear. An' there's only blanks in it. Only Stinky won't know it.

DENISE: *(As she's preparing to leave)* Franjo's certainly got the courage of his convictions.

SPIKE: He's got that arright. If The Savage Assassins catch him in make-up they'll see it as war paint.

SHOOTER: We wore make-up.

SPIKE: In the parade, not on the street.

DENISE: *(Coldly)* You wore blackface until recently.

SHOOTER: *(Defensively)* Not the same. Al Jolson wore blackface. Eddie Cantor. Regular guys. Blackface is not like lipstick... mascara.

COOKIE: *(To DENISE)* Listen honey, come back on the first. Buddy's comin home.

(SPIKE reacts to "Buddy". COOKIE continues...)

COOKIE: It's God's New Year's present to the O'Rourkes. For the novenas me an' Peaches have been sendin' up. *(To SPIKE)* Hey Spike, what if we're at the parade when he comes home? I better leave a note.

DENISE: I missed some one? Who's Buddy?

COOKIE: We all been missin' him. Trixie didn't tell ya?

SPIKE: Cookie, I don't think—

COOKIE: He was when Trixie was little.

SPIKE: Trixie's Uncle Buddy.

DENISE: You haven't seen him in a long time?

SPIKE: Vietnam. Real early on.

(DENISE nods solemnly.)

COOKIE: We didn't *see* him in Vietnam. We never been. But we sent 'im. I mean, he went 'cause he wanted to. But we gave our blessin'. Seems like only yesterday, we seen him off on a summer mornin'. He had his duffle bag... *(Reminiscing)*

DENISE: Well...what makes you think...

COOKIE: Oh, he ain't dead.

SPIKE: They found his dog tags.

COOKIE: *(Tensely)* So what! Buddy was always losin' things.

SPIKE: Officially, he's dead, Cookie.

COOKIE: *(Uncharacteristically angry)* What do officials know??? If they knew anythin', they wouldna sent him there!!! *(Cooling, to* DENISE*)* God tole me Buddy's just missin' an' he'll turn up soon. When I heard this year's theme, I kinda got upset.

SPIKE: It was that or "A Tribute To Richard Nixon".

(All wince at this.)

COOKIE: But then I figures we're honorin' all out war heroes like Buddy. An' day-by-day, I get surer an' surer the gooks are gonna spring 'im. An' he's gonna be welcomed home by twenty-two thousand Mummers.

SPIKE: *(Bitterly)* Buddy wasn't fightin' the same kinda war as previous.

COOKIE: Sure now, wasn't he fightin' for...liberty...justice. For freedom from tyranny.

SPIKE: The bill a'goods they sold us. He'd be here right now, ready to strut if I hadn't encouraged him.

COOKIE: Don't blame yerself, Spike. It was yer murmer.

DENISE: Murmer?

SPIKE: I gotta little heart murmer. Kept me outta World War Two. Tried all three branches. So, I wanted Buddy t'serve cause I didn't.

COOKIE: A natural thing, Spike.

SPIKE: I shoulda discouraged the kid. But it was real early on in Vietnam. We didn't even know where it was. But Buddy heard that they needed troops there so he signed up. And I pushed the boy. A huge mistake.

DENISE: It was the government's mistake.

COOKIE: *(Punching at the air)* Nope. "Our country, right or wrong."

SPIKE: *(Wearily)* Yeah, Cookie.

(She exits to the back room with SPIKE's *costume as she sings,* When Buddy *(nee Johnny)* Comes Marching Home, Again.*)*

SPIKE: Listen Denise, she wasn't always like this.

DENISE: I find her quite... endearing.

SPIKE: Endearin', huh? You're seein' her at her best. You oughtta see her other side. Stop around after the parade. The parade that Buddy's gonna miss again this year. The kids get my goat when they laugh at her. They don't mean no harm, of course. But Trixie an' Franjo never really knew her before Buddy's... "unaccountability". When Cookie was Trixie's age, she'd just arrived from the old country. I was shy kid with girls. So Daddy took me over to Allegheny Avenue and the Shamrock Social Club. Lots of greenhorns went there. Daddy met Momma there when she first come over.

Daddy told me to pick out a girl... ask her t'dance. But that wasn't easy for me. So he went an' brung over the prettiest dancin' partner in the hall. An' I got t'be the luckiest guy in Kensington when she took a likin' t'me. An' I got to be the luckiest guy in Philly when she married me. An' basically my luck ain't changed any...even though nowadays she's a bit...flakey...a little bit dotty.

DENISE: My grandmother got the same way. Fantasizing. Imagining things. We thought about putting her away.

SPIKE: Y'mean, like they put pets away?

DENISE: No, of course not. In an institution.

SPIKE: Well, I couldn't do that with her.

DENISE: Nor could we.

SPIKE: Good for you. An' yours.

(SHOOTER *pops up from behind the bar in his streetclothes.*)

SHOOTER: O K, Toots. Let's go!

(COOKIE *re-enters.* DENISE *gets her coat.*)

DENISE: It's been very nice, Mrs O'Rourke. I'll try to make it back post-parade.

COOKIE: Fine. But don't get your hopes up. A boy handsome as Buddy can have all the girls he wants.

DENISE: I'm sure.

COOKIE: Give us a call before ya come over. I'll put some pepper pot on.

(SPIKE *groans.*)

DENISE: (*Shaking her head*) I've never acquired a taste for...oxen's intestines.

COOKIE: It tastes better than it sounds.

(SHOOTER *whips open the door as* DENISE *exits before she gets sick.*)

SHOOTER: (*Turning to* SPIKE *and* COOKIE) Don't wait up for me. (*He starts out, then turns back*) This could be an all-nighter. (*Exit*)

COOKIE: A pretty girl.

SPIKE: A real lady. Maybe she could talk sense to Trix.

COOKIE: I got the camera loaded. I'll follow you along 'til the roll runs out. Geez, I think this is your classiest costume since *A Tribute To MASH*.

SPIKE: Two weeks with a stiff neck from that stethescope in twelve degrees.

COOKIE: It's spiffy as *The Salute To John Wayne*.

SPIKE: The year the hippies threw ice water from the rooftops in a snowstorm.

COOKIE: So ya got pneumonia. But look at the good times.

SPIKE: Fewer an' fewer. If it weren't fer Daddy, I'd've thrown in the towel years ago.

COOKIE: Spike, ya don't mean that.

SPIKE: I do. He says if I don't march I'm lettin' down the family. He says if he can march at his age, I can at mine.

COOKIE: Ah, he only gets outta the honorary car to strut for the judges.

SPIKE: He's ashamed cause I strut outta step for fancy dress. I can't play an instrument for string band. I wasn't even a funny clown.

COOKIE: Begorrah! Ignore Daddy. You're a clown, through 'n through.

SPIKE: My son-in-law thinks he married beneath himself.

COOKIE: *(Shrugging at the possibility)* Well,... us maybe. Not Peaches.

SPIKE: My grandkids are misfits 'cause I pushed the Mummers.

COOKIE: *(Her arm around him)* C'mon, Spike. I been neglectin' ya. Grab a beer. Go on upstairs. I got a pot of pepper pot.

SPIKE: I know, I know. Leave the tree on. Daddy should be back soon... I hope.

COOKIE: Spike, ya don't think that girl is innerested in Daddy?

SPIKE: I dunno. Ya never know about these young ones today.

COOKIE: I'll be up after my novena. Dig right in.

(He nods wearily and exits upstairs. COOKIE kneels to pray in front of the statue of The Virgin. She extracts a rosary and prays with eyes closed. In a moment, the wind blows the outside door open. BUDDY is nineteen years old and in summer military attire. He carries his duffle bag. She rises to close the door and sees him smiling. She is not stunned and reacts like any mother whose son has returned after an absence i.e. happily assured that he's had a safe trip.)

COOKIE: Buddy!

BUDDY: Mom!

(He drops his bag as they cross and embrace. She surveys him.)

COOKIE: You ain't changed in alla these years.

BUDDY: I'm still the same Buddy, Mom.

COOKIE: I knew you'd be. Lemmee feed you.

BUDDY: You're still the world's best cook.

COOKIE: *(Playfully)* Aw g'wan, ya little divil.

BUDDY: I'd better close the door.

COOKIE: No, don't go near the door. I don't feel no cold. An' you're warm as toast. Hey, I'll get yer dad.

BUDDY: *(Stopping her)* Wait! Not tonight. We'll surprise everyone on the first.

COOKIE: Does that mean...that you can't stay the night?

BUDDY: A day or two of debriefing. Tests. I'm not sick. A formality.

COOKIE: Well, I waited this long....

BUDDY: It'll be *our* surprise. *Our* secret.

COOKIE: *(Gleefully)* Imagine the look on their faces. *(Abruptly)* Hey, who pays for the tests? I mean, *we'll* pay if we hafta. It's just that—

BUDDY: They do, Mom.

COOKIE: It's only fair. Oh Buddy, the prices today... you can't imagine. But you'll make a good livin', now. Your trainin' as a medic.

BUDDY: I can go to college. Pre-med.

COOKIE: Oh, how I worried, Buddy. But now you're a national hero. They'll put you on T V.

BUDDY: *(Brightens)* Ed Sullivan?

COOKIE: *(Sadly)* Ed's gone. So's Loretta McLaughlin.

BUDDY: Loretta's *gone*??? Like Ed Sullivan?

COOKIE: No, no. She got married, Buddy. To Harry Mulligan.

BUDDY: Harry Mulligan??? "The Pillsbury Doughboy"?

COOKIE: They're arready divorced. But you can't marry a divorce'.

BUDDY: It's O K. She wrote me a Dear John. I was all shook up. *(Smiling blissfully)* 'Til we had R & R in Thailand.

COOKIE: But lotsa things are the same. Daddy's upstairs now, eatin' his—

BUDDY: Pepper pot! An' Peaches is happy? An' Franjo an' Trixie?

COOKIE: Peaches is happy y'know, considerin' Franjo an' Trixie.

BUDDY: An' grandpa's still kickin'?

COOKIE: You bet. Kickin' butts if he had his way.
I gotta confession t'make.

BUDDY: So, go to church.

COOKIE: I do. But the fact is, I get discouraged when God don't listen. I go deaf an' dumb t'everybody. Back in the ole country they'd say I'm "moon-tetched". Then they hafta take me t'this hospital for awhile. Your father does the night shift so he can visit every day. He brings flowers an' candy an' soon I feel like goin' to chapel. An' then things start gettin' better. I start talkin'. First to Spike. Then to others. An' then I start laughin', again. An' folks start laughin' with me... at me. I don't care. Then Spike an' Daddy can bring me home. *(Pause, smile...)* But them days are over, now.

BUDDY: You betcha. But I've gotta go, now. The captain's waiting.

COOKIE: Ohhhhh, a captain, no less. Hey Buddy, I gotta warn you. Your dad's got kinda bitter. Over the war an' what it's done to you...an' me, I guess. To all of us. He thinks Uncle Sam let us down. So don't let his ravin' an' rantin' get you dow—

BUDDY: Dad's right.

COOKIE: He is???

BUDDY: They sent us where we weren't needed and weren't wanted. Just cause a few big shots hadda have a war.

(She is dumbstruck as he kisses her gently, picks up his bag and exits. With outstretched arms, she tries to follow but the door closes mysteriously.)

COOKIE: Bye, Buddy. *(A pause...a nod to the statue)* Thanks. You know what it's like bein' a mother. *(As she heads upstairs in a hurry)* SPIKE! I GOTTA SECRET. OTHERWISE, WOULD I HAVE NEWS FOR YOU!!!

(She exits out of sight. Shortly afterwards, SHOOTER stealthily re-enters. He bumps into something and utters a mild obscenity. By the light of the Christmas tree, he crosses to the bar, sets a beer can on top of two others, retreats and whips out his gun, takes aim and fires. All three cans are blown away. Shooter cackles as he's knocked backwards over the arm of an easychair from the impact.)

SPIKE: *(Off)* Daddy, stop playin' around with that blank gun. Dinner's onna table.

SHOOTER: *(Replacing the gun on the wall and calling upstairs)* Blank gun? Sure thing, Spike. Playin' around...playin' around.

(He hobbles and cackles his way up the stairs as the lights fade out.)

END OF ACT ONE

ACT TWO

(The same, January 1, 1976, six P M)

(The den is darkened. FRANJO, PEACHES *and* COOKIE *view the T V. The tree is unlit.)*

*(*DENISE *reports the news. She could be on tape on the T V set. She could be literally "live" inside the T V frame. She could be aside—as she was at the top of* ACT ONE*—and facing the audience. Or she could be on the overhead screen or back wall.)*

(In any event, she wears a party hat and she seems engagingly inebriated since, she slurs through her report.)

NARRATOR: *(V O)* And now to Denise Walker for an on-site summary of today's Mummers' Parade. Take it away, Denise.

DENISE: Take it *away*, Morrish? Not on your life. The mummersh are here to shtay. The shpirit... the mushic...the shelebratin', the parade was all it was cracked up to be. An' for me, it wash jusht what the doctor ordered. No bull—*(Bleep)*! Lasht year at thish time I was in New York, fresh outta college and newly married. On New Yearsh Day I dishcovered that my hushband was a...TRIGAMIST!

COOKIE: Oh, dear!

PEACHES: I think she means "bigamist".

DENISE: *(Weeping)* I was one of his three wivesh.

FRANJO: That'd be a "trigamist".

DENISE: Sho he tellsh me that he'll leave the other two...if I take care of his five kids. *(Wailing)*

(From the outside, TRIXIE *enters with her characteristic slam. She joins the viewers when she's not accorded attention.* DENISE *has recovered somewhat and continues...)*

DENISE: Anyway, I'm here at parade headquarters, shubdued because of a sad footnote. For the shecond year in a row, the parade was marred by a brawl between two of the outstanding clubsh, Brotherly Love and New Quakers. But on the positive side— *(Smiling broadly)* —as befits our happy newscasht ethic—I'd say we had a draw. Although Brotherly Love was once again voted Besht Mummer's Club, New Quakersh won the post-parade fisticuffsh. So sleep it off tonight boys, secure in the knowledge that there

were no looshers. Uh...practically none. The only serious injury was
to Spike O'Rourke, son of the legendary Shooter O'Rourke who was
himshelf arrested. Fortunately, Spike is recovering from his head wound
at Fitzgerald-Mercy. So, lift one for Shpike, Philadelphia!. *(She blares a party
horn)* This is Denishe Walker, your W C A U newsperson. *(Assuming—
erroneously—that she's off the air)* God, I hate that word...*newsperson*.
(Thrusting her breasts to someone off-camera) Do these define my gender? You
betcher— *(Bleep)*. I'm all woman, not some plashtic, media, kewpie doll—

*(A "Technical Difficulties—Please Stand By" flashes.*TRIXIE *crosses and turns off
the set vehemently.* PEACHES *turns on the lights.* FRANJOs *face is battered.)*

PEACHES: Trix, T Vs are delicate mechanisms...not to be handled in a state of
pent-up aggression.

COOKIE: We gonna see the news again at eleven?

PEACHES: What're you, a masochist, Momma?

COOKIE: I dunno. I belong to a lot of organizations.

TRIXIE: I never wanna see Denise again.

PEACHES: After tonight's news, you might just get your wish.

COOKIE: Oh, she was in the holiday spirit. We need Denise to smile through
our tears. Even though Spike had a heart attack an' a concussion an'
Daddy's in jail, we can count on her.

PEACHES: Grampa's also in a state of shock.

COOKIE: Doubt it. Nothin' shocks him.
Denise almost makes me forget Bridget Mahoney. My all-time favorite
newscaster.

FRANJO: Then you couldn'a heard about Bridget an' the anchorman.

(All three women are intrigued.)

PEACHES: I didn't hear nothin'.

TRIXIE: Me, neither.

COOKIE: I heard even less.

FRANJO: Well, it's a pretty sleazy story.

PEACHES: We can take it.

TRIXIE: We're grown-ups.

*(*COOKIE *looks to* TRIXIE *with skepticism.)*

FRANJO: Member Tubby Gilligan I went t' Saint Alice's with?

PEACHES: "Tubby" Gilligan?

FRANJO: Cornelius.

PEACHES: Oh, yeah...yeah. Whatever happened t' Cornelius?

TRIXIE: He got fat, for one thing.

FRANJO: He's a bellhop at The Holiday Inn. Bridget checked in last summer with the anchorman. Stewed as prunes.

COOKIE: Dennis Perkins? One room or two?

(FRANJO *raises a finger.* COOKIE *ponders...*)

COOKIE: One bed or two?

FRANJO: Soon, the desk clerk gets a call. Perkins is staggerin' down the hall, stark naked lookin' for the ice machine.

PEACHES/COOKIE: What?/ No!

FRANJO: When the house detective knocks on their door Bridget yells, "Get lost, motha—"

(PEACHES *muffles his obscenity and slaps at* FRANJO *who disengages himself and continues...*)

FRANJO: Hey, I didn't say it. Tubby said it. I mean, Tubby said that Bridget said it.

PEACHES: I don't care who said it.

COOKIE: This all started the day you let him transfer to public school. *(Pointing to* TRIXIE*)* And when this one left Mercy Academy.

TRIXIE: I *graduated*! When you graduate you leave.

COOKIE: In three years you graduated. Cause you were smart.

TRIXIE: No, motivated. Mercy was merciless.
Then what happened, Fran?

FRANJO: So, when the cop got the door open, Bridget—also naked—
let fly with a bottle of vodka. When it missed, she kicked him right inna b—
...right inna groin. Then Tubby rushes in an' grabs her. *(Laughs)* I tole Tubby that's as close as he'll ever get to a naked lady.

TRIXIE: *You* said that to *him*? That's rich.

PEACHES: I don't believe it.

FRANJO: You know Tubby, Ma. He's too dumb to lie.

COOKIE: That's just celebrity gossip. Why wasn't it on the news, Mister Smarty Pants?

(A thump from off. COOKIE *reacts.)*

COOKIE: That must be Buddy. He's overdue.

(TRIXIE *scurries out the door and returns with a* Philadelphia Bulletin. *The headline: "Mummers March Marred By Mayhem!")*

TRIXIE: I nearly didn't come home today, I was so scared.

PEACHES: What's your excuse for last night?

TRIXIE: Oh...I was...I felt tension in the air. So I stayed put.

PEACHES: Put where? You stayed out all night.

TRIXIE: I stayed *in*. Wouldn't you want that on a cold winter night?

PEACHES: In your friend Steve's apartment?

TRIXIE: I was safe. He wasn't a mummer.

PEACHES: Don't tell your father. He'll press charges against this boy. Corrupting a child.

TRIXIE: I'm *not* a child!

PEACHES: Your father hasn't noticed. We were worried about you.

TRIXIE: About me? I'm the least of your worries. I just left Grandpa in the hospital. He's gonna be alright, Grandma.

COOKIE: So they told us. But they wouldn't let us visit. Hey... how'd you get in to see Spike?

TRIXIE: Snuck in. Then I went an' saw Shooter.

COOKIE: An' surely they'll be lettin' him out of jail?

TRIXIE: Daddy's bailed him out. If they put Shooter in the slammer he'd be a menace to hardened criminals.

FRANJO: *(Grabbing the paper)* Is my picture in there?

TRIXIE: Look in the cartoons, jerkeroo.

COOKIE: Oh, looka the gesture that girl is makin' at the camera.

FRANJO: Says here she's a member of "The Neo-radical Feminist Coalition."

COOKIE: She don't look very feminine.

FRANJO: *(Reading)* Quote, "The disruption should bring an end to this sexist parade. It is simply a reiteration of the fact that without the stabilizing and pacifying influence of women in leadership positions in all areas of society, men will resort to their traditional barbarism. Fortunately, the casualties were exclusively male... as is fitting."

COOKIE: ..."leadership positions in all areas of society"...? What's she wanna be, head coach of The Eagles?

FRANJO: I think she'd line The Eagles up against a wall and shoot 'em.

COOKIE: After last season, so would Spike.

PEACHES: Exactly what happened to cause the riot?

FRANJO: Well, it was about a mile after we passed you...

COOKIE: I got pitchers. In color.

FRANJO: Shooter's at the head of Brotherly Love in the convertible. We're struttin' away, hunkey-dorey when five shots ring out. I figure black people are attackin' since we're at Broad an' South. But when the dust clears, I look up an' there's Shooter in the open convertible wavin' a pistol while five New Quakers are clutchin' their asses.

PEACHES: I saw trouble, lettin' Brotherly Love march behind New Quakers.

FRANJO: Well, the Quakers storm our ranks but we fight 'em off. (He re-enacts with macho exaggeration) I deck one guy with an uppercut, another with a right cross. I heard his jaw crack. Hit another so hard with a left, he was beggin' for a right.

TRIXIE: You talk like Muhammed Ali. You look like you welched on a bet with Scarfazio.

FRANJO: Then the black people start throwin' bricks from their rooftops.

COOKIE: They're a peculiar people, keepin' bricks on their rooftops.

FRANJO: Soon, mummers from all the other clubs are fightin' with one another. Shooter is bein' carted off to the hoosegow. So, I find Pop and Grandpop an' I says, "Let's get outta here!"

TRIXIE: Smart thinkin'!!!

FRANJO: But Pop's gotta go t'the station house for Shooter. So me'n Grandpop run inta the subway. Only we don't have any money 'causa the costumes.

COOKIE: Next year, I'll sew pockets.

FRANJO: So, I leap over the turnstile and onta the train. I turn for Grandpop but his leap doesn't quite clear. And he tumbles and lands on his head. But before I can hop out an' rescue him, the doors close. I shoulda got off at the next stop...gone back. But who knew? Grandpop always staggers home no matter his condition.

TRIXIE: (Reading the paper) Next year you'll sew pockets, huh Grandma?

COOKIE: Can't give men purses. An' they're men among men.

TRIXIE: There won't be a next year.

FRANJO: WHAT???

TRIXIE: *(Shoving the paper at him)* "Two Clubs Banned Permanently From Mummer's Parade!"

FRANJO: Oh no, I can't read this.

COOKIE: Hey, what's wrong with you, boy? What is it Spike says when he watches The Phillies?

PEACHES: "Get rid of the bum"???

COOKIE: No, no..."Hang in there!" *(Reading)* "Harold Morgan, President of The Mummers Association made the following statement in the wake of today's disruption." —Wake is right.— "On behalf of the tremendous percentage of law-abiding Mummers, I would like to announce that Brotherly Love and New Quakers are hereafter banned from any future parades. Despite their proud achievements, their behavior is inconsistent with their accomplishments. It is with regards to the safety of all citizens that we must sever ties with both organizations."

FRANJO: Oh, no. They can't do this. I'm just gettin' started.

TRIXIE: Stop your bellyachin', Franjo.

FRANJO: I work my way up to fancy dress so I can...well, express myself an' they pull the rug out from under me.
I AM NOT RESPONSIBLE FOR THAT OLE BASTARD, SHOOTER O'ROURKE!!!

PEACHES: FRANCIS JOSEPH CATANIA! HOW DARE YOU!!!

COOKIE: Hey, here's Spike's name. "Jeremiah O'Rourke, the son of Shooter O'Rourke, suffered a minor concussion and a slight heart attack when he tried to beat the fare on the Broad St. subway." The paper called him "Jeremiah". Spike'll have a *massive* heart attack.

FRANJO: God, my whole career wiped out. I'm obsolete. Like a do-do bird.

TRIXIE: Not obsolete, Fran. There's always room for another do-do.

FRANJO: Are you tryna be funny?

TRIXIE: Am I tryna be funny says Bozo The Clown.

(FRANJO starts after her. She wards him off with a barstool.)

PEACHES: Cut it out? Can't you stop fightin' on a night like this?

COOKIE: Like onna box of salt. "When it rains it pours."

(All stare. COOKIE elaborates...)

COOKIE: Y'know, the little girl with the umbrella?

TRIXIE: Sorry, Ma.

FRANJO: Me too, Ma.

PEACHES: I'm at my wit's end keeping order in this family. A normal woman—

TRIXIE: *(Respectfully)* You're not normal, Ma.

PEACHES: WHAT???

TRIXIE: *(Genuinely defensive)* I mean...you're not average! Not typical! You're special!!!

PEACHES: It's too late for discipline. So much for permissive child rearing.

COOKIE: Yer mom's right, Trix. Yer gettin' too spoiled for yer britches.

TRIXIE: What about Franjo?

COOKIE: Franjo's different. We never expected much from him.

(FRANJO deflates. COOKIE continues...)

COOKIE: But you...you're special. Smart...pretty. Yer daddy's little girl. He buys you a car... clothes...summer in Italy. *(Irritably)* Just to get our goat.

TRIXIE: Hey Grandma, I appreciate what's been done for me.

COOKIE: Then why so cynical, honey? At nineteen. That I'd be likin' t'know. Ya don't believe in God...

TRIXIE: I never said I didn't believe in God. I just have trouble with his church.

COOKIE: Ya don't believe in your family.

TRIXIE: I believe in my family. I just have trouble with the individuals.

COOKIE: You don't believe in the mummers.

TRIXIE: *(Shrugs)* Two out of three ain't bad.

FRANJO: You coulda seen me make my fancy dress debut.

TRIXIE: You know I don't go anymore. I was schlepped off to fifteen parades before my 15th birthday. I watched those guys strut half-crocked up Broad St. while I'm freezin' my ass off onna sidelines. Finally I ask myself, "Where am I in the scheme of this lunacy." I swore that was my last parade. A New Year's resolution that's a cinch to keep. By the way Fran, I *did* see ya on T V sittin' in front of a fireplace drinkin' a scotch and soda.

COOKIE: Franjo wasn't in fronta a fireplace drinkin' a scotch and so-

TRIXIE: I was in front of a fireplace!!! God, Grandma, your mind is like a banana republican.

(PEACHES stares at her. TRIXIE withdraws.)

FRANJO: Who were you sittin' an' drinkin' *with*?

TRIXIE: A friend.

FRANJO: Anybody I know?

TRIXIE: If *you* knew him, he wouldn't be my friend.

FRANJO: What's his name?

TRIXIE: It's irrelevant. Do I ever ask you about *your* friends?

FRANJO: Y'know I don't have any.

TRIXIE: *(Suddenly touched...after a beat)* Hey Fran, ya looked great. No kiddin'. Maybe a little too much make-up but otherwise-

FRANJO: You can go to extremes in fancy dress division. How about Sons Of Liberty Club comin' as Father Time. Now, that's extreme.

COOKIE: Each man made up as a clock.

TRIXIE: *(Twirling her finger at her temple)* Coo-coo...coo-coo.

FRANJO: Synchronized, too. Each clock read three-seventeen.

PEACHES: Not exactly synchronized, Fran. They read three-seventeen at noon.

TRIXIE: Wait, I think I hear a car comin' up the driveway.

COOKIE: It's Buddy!!! *(Rushing to peer out, then in dismay...)* It's the cops.

(A whirling red light reflects from outside. COOKIE suddenly panics.)

COOKIE: Franjo! They're here for you! For fightin'. Inta the bathroom!!! Behind the shower curtain.

(Without even thinking, FRANJO obeys. When he's off, COOKIE turns to TRIXIE...)

COOKIE: Stay away from that window, Trix. There might be a bullet with your named on it!!! That's how they say it on T V. Also, "cement booties". They say that, too.

O S VOICE: O K, gentlemen. Get a good night's sleep. It's all over.

GASPARI: *(Off)* Thanks officer, I appreciate all your help.

O S VOICE: Don't forget your top hat, old timer.

GASPARI: *(Off)* I'll take it for him.

(PEACHES opens the door. SHOOTER enters, shuffling slowly. He seems in shock. PEACHES aids him. GASPARI enters, unconcerned. Both their costumes are disheveled. GASPARI's backpiece is missing.)

GASPARI: *(Waving out the door)* Good night, now.

O S VOICE: Happy New Year.

GASPARI: *(Quietly bitter, as he closes the door)* Wise guy!

(The red light fades. SHOOTER *staggers listlessly, his jaw dangling. All but* GASPARI *and* TRIXIE—*who is trying to secretly suppress a giggle*—*survey him with various degrees of pity.* FRANJO *emerges guardedly from the bathroom.)*

PEACHES: *(Apprehensively)* Yo, Gramps.

*(*SHOOTER *tries vainly to react.* COOKIE *whips out her rosary beads and prays silently as* GASPARI *pours a stiff drink.)*

GASPARI: How 'bout a couple of beers, Shooter? Cap off the day.

PEACHES: GASPARI!

GASPARI: Too bad you were arrested. You were on your way to a snootful.

PEACHES: Hey Gas, the old guy's in shock.

GASPARI: He doesn't know the meaning of the word.

SHOOTER: Yo...Yo...Yo... *(As he shambles to the window)*

PEACHES: Yo, Grandpa. C'mon,... Yo—

SHOOTER: Yo...Yo... *(Looking out the window)*

PEACHES: Now how d'you feel, Franjo? After the terrible thing you said about your grandfather?

SHOOTER: *(Suddenly, his old self again)* Yo Dem Golden Slippers. *(Singing and strutting as pandemonium breaks loose)* Yo Dem Golden Slippers.

*(*TRIXIE *is doubled over with laughter,* GASPARI *is blasé and the others are shocked.* COOKIE *raises her clasped hands heavenward.)*

SHOOTER: *(After a brief strut)* That was a humdinger. Like the old days. Only thing missin' was my horse. The things you can get away with when you're my age.

*(*GASPARI *hands him a beer)*

SHOOTER: Thanks, Gas-par-i. Tell 'em about me down at the station house.

GASPARI: Strictly Academy Award.

SHOOTER: Damn right. You cried yerself 'til I told you I was fakin' it.

GASPARI: That's a lie. The cops cried. But I didn't.

SHOOTER: It's my playactin' that got me sprung.

GASPARI: You mean my legal expertise.

SHOOTER: You mean I'm beholden to ya?

*(*GASPARI *nods.* SHOOTER *continues...)*

SHOOTER: Am I gonna get a bill?

*(*GASPARI *nods.* SHOOTER *continues [imploringly]...)*

SHOOTER: Aw, g'wan. We're family. You'd present a bill to a loved one? Gaspari, my boy, say it isn't so.

GASPARI: Eat your heart out.

COOKIE: *(Sobbing)* Thank God, you're arright.

SHOOTER: Cut the water works, baby. Spike's comin' along, huh?

PEACHES: He'd gonna be arright with plenty of rest.

COOKIE: His murmer's makin' itself heard.

PEACHES: You better look for a new day man.

SHOOTER: *(Nods, then to* COOKIE*)* I'll send you an' Spike to Florida. Poor guy. It's all my fault.

COOKIE: Spike don't hold no grudge.

SHOOTER: He's a fine lad, my boy. But he ain't a real trooper. When he struts, the kick's not there. Never had it that I can remember.

COOKIE: Bite yer tongue, Daddy. You done nothin' but ridicule him—

SHOOTER: Aw, pipe down. I just—

COOKIE: SHUT UP, DADDY!!! I GOT THE FLOOR!!!

*(Shocked silence from everyone. The family members will attempt to intervene—*PEACHES *in particular—but she is not to be silenced and her behavior may border on insanity as* COOKIE *continues...)*

COOKIE: He's put in over forty years behind the stick fer you. Ya work 'im sixty-seventy hours a week. Since he's the only one you can trust. Never any O T. He's always wanted t'make you proud but all you ever done was mock 'im. We coulda moved...had a place of our own. Modest, of course, since you don't pay well. After Buddy was missin', we wanted t'start a new life. Away from here. Spike wouldn't hafta listen t'the T V and the customers talk about the war. But no, you insisted we stay 'cause you were gettin' old an' the joint would fall apart. So we seen our dreams go down the ole drain. We hung around cause it kept you alive. Now, it's too late for us. Spike took care a'you alla these years. Now you hafta take care a'Spike. *(Winding down, drained by the outburst)* Naw, Spike's a trouper. The best there is. Alla these years, he thought it was his fault you didn't recognize him for what he was. But it ain't his fault! No, sirree. It's *your* fault.

*(*SHOOTER *feigns tears.* COOKIE's *undeterred...)*

CUT IT OUT, DADDY! IT WON'T WORK NO MORE!!!

SHOOTER: *(Realizing that "it won't work no more", he sobers...)* I didn't mean no harm. It's just like Spike's a big teddy bear.

COOKIE: Well, he's a big teddy bear with a bum ticker, now. *(She retreats near the outside door. Soon, she'll slip out unnoticed.)*

GASPARI: *(To* PEACHES*)* Has she been taking her tranquilizers?

SHOOTER: *(Interjecting)* Yeah. But when she feels strong about somethin', they don't work.

PEACHES: *(Trying to change the subject)* What's the disposition?

GASPARI: Lousy.

PEACHES: The disposition of Grandpa's case.

GASPARI: The disposition is the verdict.

PEACHES: Can the jargon. Spill the beans.

GASPARI: Released on his own recognizance. Probably a suspended sentence. That old pistol didn't pack much punch. Superficial wounds. Besides, they need a weapon to prosecute. And it's disappeared.

*(*FRANJO *takes the gun from his costume and holds it up, proudly.)*

SHOOTER: *(Lunging for the gun)* Yippee! I'm a free man!

FRANJO: *(Holding the gun at bay)* Well, whataya say t'me, Shooter?

SHOOTER: I say, what wuzzit you said about me? Yer mother just told you t'spit it out an' you clammed up like -

FRANJO: I'm sorry. I flew off the handle.

SHOOTER: You live in a beautiful house in the suburbs...money, clothes, comforts. What d'you have to fly offa—

FRANJO: I was mad at you cause we got kicked outta the parade.

SHOOTER: We'll get 'em next year.

FRANJO: There ain't no next year.

SHOOTER: There's always a next year.

COOKIE: Morgan kicked us out. Us an' New Quakers.

SHOOTER: That son of a bitch! Hoagie, why didn't tell me?

GASPARI: *(Pouring another strong drink)* Believe it or not, I was busy.

FRANJO: So, I apologize for callin' you... *(Tearfully)* A miserable old bastard.

SHOOTER: That's all? That's not a curse. That's a fact. *(To no one in particular)* Lemmee think of a way around this predicament.

TRIXIE: Best thing that ever happened to us.

GASPARI: Hardly. My name associated with common street brawlers. My reputation besmirched at the country club.

PEACHES: They didn't ask if we were mummers on the application.

GASPARI: They abhor mummers. We're ludicrous to them.

TRIXIE: If the shoe fits-

SHOOTER: Yer Main Line neighbors didn't jump for joy when you slapped "Catania" on the mailbox. And your country club is nothin' more'n a Knights of Columbus Hall with a golf course.

GASPARI: It's an exclusive club.

SHOOTER: It's exclusive, arright. Every member's been rejected elsewhere. You play golf with "Mushy" Hanlon?

GASPARI: Marty Hanlon? T Martin Hanlon, III? Stocks and bonds.

SHOOTER: Well, it was Mushy when he was comin' up in Kensington. He pay his bills at yer club?

GASPARI: Certainly. He's never been posted.

SHOOTER: Well, he posted me t'the wall for two hundred and seventy-five dollars before he moved. I couldn't let his mother pay his tab outta her pension. *(He turns away, then back to GASPARI)* When you courted Peaches you didn't put on airs. Don't forget where you come from. You're descended from a great culture.

(Touched, GASPARI puts his arm around SHOOTER who continues...)

SHOOTER: Not as great as *our* culture, but—

TRIXIE: I tell ya, Pop. In the long run it'll do us good.

GASPARI: No, not this notoriety. I've spent years trying to provide my family with a life of comfort and respectability. Even after law school, I've kept up. *(To PEACHES)* Remember those self-improvement courses, Babe?

PEACHES: Your self-improvement nearly destroyed me. Remember the elocution course and the night you swallowed the marble?

GASPARI: It paid off. *(To TRIXIE)* No Angel, you're going to have to tighten your belt. Lean times lie ahead. Prosperity's a thing of the pa - *(He stares at her for a long moment)* Where the hell were you these last twenty-four hours?

TRIXIE: *(Timidly)* Celebratin'.

GASPARI: Celebrating what?

SHOOTER: Whattaya think, The Second Coming? *(Crossing to the bathroom)*

GASPARI: Where were you celebrating?

TRIXIE: Downtown. A friend's place.

GASPARI: What friend? I know what goes on at these all-night parties.

TRIXIE: Some guy.

GASPARI: Well, that eliminates half the world.

TRIXIE: Forty-nine percent! *We're* the majority.

GASPARI: Who's this guy?

TRIXIE: Steve.

GASPARI: Steve?

PEACHES: Trix, how come ya never brought this fella home t'meet us?

TRIXIE: Cause I like him. I bring home the creeps.

FRANJO: Ya sure do.

TRIXIE: Gives Franjo someone he can relate to.

PEACHES: *(Suddenly alarmed)* Hey, hey where's Momma?

(She crosses and opens the bathroom door. SHOOTER bellows. Everyone but GASPARI starts looking for her. He pours another drink. PEACHES calls upstairs. FRANJO looks outside.)

FRANJO: Hey, she's at the end of the driveway. *(He exits.)*

PEACHES: *(Solemnly to TRIXIE)* It's startin' again.

TRIXIE: Maybe when Grandpa comes home-

PEACHES: It's not Grandpa she's lookin' for.

(SHOOTER emerges pugnaciously.)

SHOOTER: Hey, what's the big idea?

PEACHES: Not now, Gramps. We were lookin' for Momma.

SHOOTER: Find 'er?

(TRIXIE nods, points outside. SHOOTER continues...)

SHOOTER: Last time, she took a bus t' 30th St. station in a sweater in the middle of winter.

(FRANJO and COOKIE enter. She is shivering. They put TRIXIE's jacket over her shoulders.)

PEACHES: You O K, Momma?

COOKIE: Sure. Couldn't be happier. Just impatient.

GASPARI: Look Cookie, I'll personally take you to see Spike tomorrow. Now, if we can all relax...calm down...count our blessings. Steve who, Trix?

TRIXIE: Steve *Grossman.*

GASPARI: *(Appalled, to* PEACHES*)* GROSSMAN!!! Another twist of the knife for her middle-aged, middle-class parents. What do hopeless squares like us know?

PEACHES: I'm not a square. *(Shrugs)* I'm not a swinger, but...

GASPARI: *(To* TRIXIE*)* You spent the *entire night* with this Grossman?

TRIXIE: No, he let me sleep in his car. At dawn he came and carried me upstairs, held me over the fireplace to thaw—

GASPARI: You've just gone too far! What's his number?

TRIXIE: Wait a minute.

GASPARI: Covering up this all-night party? I see these demented, drug-ridden kids down at the lock-up.

TRIXIE: Daddy, we just sat around singin' Christmas carols.

GASPARI: Christmas was last week!!!

*(*SHOOTER *is drifting off.)*

TRIXIE: Steve wouldn't know that.

PEACHES: Give Dad his number, hon. You know him when he gets like this. He'll track the boy down and make a citizen's arrest.

TRIXIE: 487-2803.

COOKIE: *(Joyously)* It must be serious. She memorized the number.

TRIXIE: I can't believe this. Look Pop, I'll give you all of last night's details, step-by-step.

GASPARI: Does it never end? Now you want to regale us with details.

PEACHES: *(Taking Trixie aside)* You know you can't beat around the bush with your father.

TRIXIE: I'm not still playin' spin the bottle. He doesn't want the truth.

PEACHES: He's got a legal mind. Criminality is what you get arrested for. Anythin' else is sin.

GASPARI: Hello, Grossman? This is Gaspari Catania, Attorney-At-Law. Huh?... Well, put him on, please. *(To the others)* His roommate.

COOKIE: I'm prayin' for ya, honey.

TRIXIE: *(Wearily)* For what, Grandma?

COOKIE: For the lesser evil.

GASPARI: Grossman? Gaspari Cartania, Attorney-At-Law. How do you do? I'd like to ask a straightforward question of you. An honest response would be appreciated... Of course not. You're not under oath. It just happens that I'm an attorney.... *(Smiles proudly)* Oh, she did, huh? She mentioned I was Law Review editor, huh? *(Winks at* TRIXIE*)* Good. Alright, here's the sixty-four dollar question. Ready? What transpired at your all-night party? ...WHAT?... No all-night party? *(Looking to* TRIXIE *with dead seriousness)* Don't cover up, Grossman. I'd have the vice squad there in two minutes if it weren't for my daughter... You stick to your guns? *(To* TRIXIE*)* He says he wasn't even with you.

TRIXIE: Naturally, he's gonna say that. Can I talk to him?

GASPARI: *(To* TRIXIE*)* It was a drug orgy. You don't *remember* who you were with.

PEACHES: Let 'er speak t'the kid. Maybe there's a misunderstanding.

TRIXIE: *(Grabbing the phone)* Steve... look Steve, get hold of yourself.

GASPARI: *(To* PEACHES*)* There's sincerity in that boy's voice. Not like Trixie's voice.

TRIXIE: *(Into the phone)* Settle down and tell the truth.

GASPARI: Where'd we go wrong, Peaches?

TRIXIE: *(Holding out the phone)* Pop...

GASPARI: Too late. The boy's confessed. You're indicted.

TRIXIE: But he's got somethin' else to say.

PEACHES: Talk to him again, Gaspari.

GASPARI: For you I'll talk to him, Peaches. Not for her. *(Into the phone)* Grossman? Catania, here... You what? ... No, you weren't under oath. But it's a matter of ethics. Common courtesy...I see... Just the two of you. No drugs?... Champagne. That's acceptable... T V at midnight. Times Square. A real nuthouse, huh?.. Lit the fireplace. Practical move with today's heating costs. Just like you people to think of that.

*(*TRIXIE *and* PEACHES *groan [silently].* GASPARI *continues...)*

GASPARI: Danced awhile? *(Smiles...giggles)* With a phone book between you?... Nothing. A parochial school joke... never mind.... Finished the champagne... Woozy... *(Nervously)* Laid down on the convertable sofa.

(The women are nervous. COOKIE *prays.* GASPARI *continues...)*

GASPARI: Must've been a tight squeeze...I see. You converted the sofa.

TRIXIE: *(Shouting into the phone)* WRAP IT UP, STEVE!

GASPARI: *(Nervously)* Then you drifted off?... "Eventually"??? Well, "eventually" is good enough for me... Let's leave it at "eventually"... Good.

You love my daughter! *Well, so do I!!!*... Now, go back to doing what kids do today. Meditating...chanting...

TRIXIE: Wait, lemmee talk to him. *(Grabbing the phone)* Steve, say something.

GASPARI: *(To* PEACHES, *confidently)* Don't worry, honey. Strictly platonic.

PEACHES: Platonic? He said that?

GASPARI: He implied it. I determined it in that sincere voice. Don't worry. Our little Trixie is still... "Our Little Trixie".

*(*PEACHES *looks skeptical as* GASPARI *pours himself a tall one and continues...)*

GASPARI: How 'bout a drink, Son?

FRANJO: Thought you'd never ask.

COOKIE: Watch that, Hoagie. You're not used to it.

GASPARI: Maybe I'm assimilating... God forbid.

(He pours for his son.)

TRIXIE: *(Quietly into the phone)* Jeffrey? What happened?... He fainted again? Like when the North Gym security guard caught us a four A M on the trampoline?... Yeah, have him call.

TRIXIE: *(Hangs up, then to her father)* Satisfied?

GASPARI: I suppose so. Considering the alternative.

SHOOTER: *(Popping awake)* I got it!

PEACHES: Ya got what, Gramps?

SHOOTER: It came t'me inna dream.

COOKIE: What did?

SHOOTER: The answer.

COOKIE: Like answers come t'the saints in dreams?

TRIXIE: Is that supposed to be an analogy?

SHOOTER: T'hell with Brotherly Love. We'll start over. New club. New name.

PEACHES: You'll never get away with it.

SHOOTER: I won't march. I'm startin' to slow down. I'll just back a new club. The brains behind the scene.

TRIXIE: Who'd lead?

SHOOTER: Spike!

COOKIE: Not on yer life!

SHOOTER: You speakin' for Spike?

COOKIE: In no uncertain terms!

SHOOTER: So be it. Scratch Spike. Hoagie, if you'll cancel today's legal bill, I'll allow you to—

GASPARI: When the moon turns to green cheese.

SHOOTER: Ingrate! *(Beat)* Who's left?

(FRANJO is desperately trying to draw attention to himself.)

TRIXIE: Forget it, Fran. They ban the clubs, they ban the marchers.

PEACHES: I dunno. Morgan didn't say nothin' about the marchers.

SHOOTER: Forget Morgan. I marched before he was born. I gotta few strings.

FRANJO: What about *me* leadin'? Even if the marchers are banned, nobody knows what I look like. And since my name's Catania, nobody'll know I was related to Shooter.

SHOOTER: Hmmm, that's a point. *(Ponders)* Nah, you're too young. Besides, you're too fruity.

GASPARI: *(Drunkenly)* THERE'S NOTHING WRONG WITH MY BOY!!!

FRANJO: There is! There is! And you created this condition. You all did.

GASPARI: It's the liquor gettin' t'you, boy. *(Tipsily, his arm slips off the bar)*

FRANJO: You send me t'that shrink. Sixty bucks an hour.

GASPARI: He'sh the best there is. Belongs to the club.

TRIXIE: He don't wanna deal with my problems. Just my sex life.

PEACHES: What d'ya tell him???

GASPARI: *(Panicky)* This is not the time nor the plache—

PEACHES: *(To GASPARI)* It's never time for you to talk with Franjo!
(To FRANJO) What d'ya tell 'im?

FRANJO: Nothin'.

GASPARI: At sixty dollars an hour, tell 'im somethin'. Anythin'. Tell 'im a joke.

FRANJO: *(To PEACHES)* I tell 'im I don't have a sex life.

GASPARI: *(Cheerfully)* See, my boy's alright.

TRIXIE: At his age? What's alright about that?

GASPARI: Trix, maybe you can fix him up with a co-ed who's got a...y' know, reputat—

(TRIXIE glares, GASPARI quiets.)

PEACHES: Well, what does the shrink say?

FRANJO: He asks if I want a sex life.

GASPARI: Well... *(A long sip for fortification)* ...do you?

FRANJO: Certainly, I do. Don't you?

COOKIE: Franjo, is that any way to talk to your daddy???

GASPARI: *(Fearfully)* With...with anyone in particular?

FRANJO: With Mary Jane Ciparelli! If she'd only notice me!

GASPARI: *(Elated)* Mary Jane! MARY JANE!!! MARY JANE CIPARELLI, no less!!! Twice blessed! TWICE BLESSED!!!

TRIXIE: *(Sincerely)* I'll put in a good word for ya, Fran.

GASPARI: That creepy psychiatrist. I'll cancel payment on that last check.

FRANJO: He always called me "Francis". Never Franjo.

SHOOTER: Never name a boy "Francis".

TRIXIE: Shooter, we're in the process of uninhibiting my brother's libido.

FRANJO: Actually—except for the lack of it—my problem's not sex. It's attire. You guys indoctrinated me. Now you gotta help the monster you created.

COOKIE: Mummer. Not monster.

FRANJO: I've got an identity crises. I've never known who I was. Only on New Year's Day. It felt great to be special... an' a winner.

SHOOTER: Betcher ass.

FRANJO: I'm over-obsessed with *your* obsession. So I put on costumes an' make-up an' strut through the streets in the wee hours.

PEACHES: You ruined that kimono we bought in Japan.

TRIXIE: An' that Italian knit shawl from last summer.

FRANJO: So, what about my costume addiction? How will I earn a livin'. Playin' Santa Claus?

COOKIE: That's seasonal. How 'bout a clown?

SHOOTER: You got a head start.

FRANJO: So, let's cut a deal that'll make everyone happy. Includin' me. I'll only strut one day a year if I can lead Shooter's new club. So what if I'm too young? If you're gonna form a new club, Shooter, form a *new* club. Throw out the old rules. Let everyone join who wants to join.

SHOOTER: *(Pondering)* That'd be a boot in Morgan's ass, wouldn't it?

TRIXIE: Women???

FRANJO: Why not?

SHOOTER: I got nothin' against girls marchin'. Why, in the ole days—

GASPARI: We know...we know...we heard.

SHOOTER: Ya did? Who told ya?

COOKIE: If God wanted lady mummers, he'd 'a made 'em. I say veto that....

SHOOTER: We could have women. I always thought we could have anyone who could strut or clown or musicalize. Y' know, if James Bland came back, he wouldn'a been in today's parade.

FRANJO: Who's James Bland?

COOKIE: Y'see, these kids today, Daddy... no sense a' history. James Bland wrote our theme song, "Oh Dem Golden Slippers".

FRANJO: Why wouldn't he have been in today's parade?

COOKIE: He's dead.

SHOOTER: Naw, naw, Cookie. He was colored. That's why.

(Surprise all around. SHOOTER continues...)

SHOOTER: It's true. I knew Jimmy.

FRANJO: Then let's open the club up. How 'bout you, Ma? You strut better at the parties than any of the guys. Look better, too.

PEACHES: *(Tempted for a moment)* Uh...nah. Thanks, but no thanks.

FRANJO: Trixie, what about your rights as a woman?

TRIXIE: That right I'll forfeit. But you, Ma. Get outta the sewin' room.

PEACHES: Who'd make the costumes?

FRANJO: We'd hold auditions. Those who can't strut or clown or play an instrument could do the dirty work.

COOKIE: Y'mean, men? It'd never work.

PEACHES: I must admit, I always had a secret desire t'march.

COOKIE: Peaches! For shame.

FRANJO: Think about it, Ma.

TRIXIE: Shooter's got the dough to start a new club.

FRANJO: An' the connections.

SHOOTER: An' the sympathy of the public. They dunno I'm a dirty ole man.

PEACHES: *(Warming up to the notion)* It sure would upset the apple cart.

GASPARI: *(Blotto by now)* Franjo, my son. I never had any doubts about you.

FRANJO: Nor me about you, Dad.

(GASPARI *doesn't quite know what to make of this as the door flies open and* DENISE *staggers in. She wears an overcoat and* GASPARI's *helmet and she plays a sad facsimile of "Golden Slippers" on a party horn. She struts around the room.*)

TRIXIE: Denise!

THE OTHERS: DENISE*!!!*

DENISE: Happy New Year.

SHOOTER: Hiya, Toots. Our T V interview turned out pretty good.

DENISE: You were great. People are buzzing about your appearance the other night.

PEACHES: They're buzzin' about his appearance today, too.

SHOOTER: Yeah, I got five New Quakers right inna ass.

TRIXIE: What're you doin' here?

DENISE: Partyin' the night away!

PEACHES: After what we've been through, you've come to party?

DENISE: It was Spike's idea.

COOKIE: You seen Spike?

DENISE: Seen 'im? I got 'im.

(SPIKE *enters in his topcoat over a hospital gown. His head is wrap-around bandaged and he has his clothes over his arm.* DENISE *struts to the bar for a drink.*)

COOKIE: SPIKE*!!!*

(*All the others shout simultaneously* ["Daddy" *or* "Gramps" *or* "Spike"]*.*)

SPIKE: Pipe down, will ya? I gotta headache.

COOKIE: *(Embracing him)* A miracle! A miracle!

SPIKE: A miracle? A little pain in the chest. A little bump on my bean.

COOKIE: You look like the drummer boy.

(*All look to her.* COOKIE *elaborates...*)

COOKIE: Y'know, "Spirit of '76". How appropriate. *(Rethinks for a moment)* Or was it the flute boy?

PEACHES: Pop, yer supposed to be inna hospital.

SPIKE: What? An' miss the party?

PEACHES: *(Turning on* DENISE*)* Are you responsible for this?

SPIKE: Relax. She come t' visit me. I asked her t'spring me. She wouldn't bite 'til I told 'er I was goin' over the wall.

DENISE: I figured I'd drive Spike rather than let him take the subway.

FRANJO: He's probably been banned from the subway.

SPIKE: Besides, the doc said I could go home. He just didn't say when.

(SPIKE, DENISE *and* SHOOTER *laugh at this. She has an arm around* SPIKE's *shoulder.* COOKIE *removes it in no uncertain terms.*)

(*Suddenly,* SPIKE *grimaces.*)

COOKIE: It hurts?

SPIKE: Only when I laugh.

PEACHES: (*Irritably*) Hey Denise, ya still got a job t'go back to after tonight?

DENISE: Nope, I just got fired. But I don't care. Hey Hoagie, how 'bout a drink?

GASPARI: (*Crossing blindly and handing her a business card*) Gaspari Catania, Esquire. You may need this as an accomplice to Spike's escape.

(*She tosses the card, lightly.*)

SPIKE: Hey, somebody gimmee a beer.

COOKIE: Oh, I dunno.

(*But* FRANJO *delivers a can as* GASPARI *is dialing the phone.*)

SPIKE: Hey, what's this I hear we got kicked outta the parade?

PEACHES: We're startin' a new club.

SHOOTER: I'll let Franjo lead the new club. I'll call the shots from behind the scenes.

FRANJO: HOT DAMN!!!

SHOOTER: Relax, boy. I'm still the godfather in this outfit.

GASPARI: (*To* DENISE) What heretofore hidden benevolence prompted a visit to Shpike?

DENISE: I dunno. I've been away from home for a long time. It's New Years. I'm alone in a new town. I miss my folks...grandparents, especially.

TRIXIE: What does Spike have in common—

DENISE: And Cookie.

TRIXIE: ...with *your* grandparents?

COOKIE: Well, they got history. They probably squabble some. Complain a lot about changes-

DENISE: And been married fifty-two years.

COOKIE: *(Somewhat dismayed)* We've only been forty-four.

DENISE: And there's vitality here. Not my kind of vitality but you take it where you can get it.

SHOOTER: *(Indicating the others)* Yeah, they're real cut-ups.

(She plants a kiss on SHOOTER's head. He lunges for her.)

SHOOTER: Hey you can do better than that.

(She scurries away.)

GASPARI: *(Into the phone)* Hello, 9-1-1. This is Gaspari Catania, Attorney-At-Law. I'd like to report a kidnapping... Yeah, I can hold.

(SHOOTER retrieves the gun from wherever FRANJO placed it. PEACHES and COOKIE start to panic but smiling FRANJO produces a handful of bullets. But his father hasn't seen the ammunition. Nor has DENISE.)

SHOOTER: Hang up the phone, Hoagie.

GASPARI: *(Surprised to say the least)* Whaaaa...

SHOOTER: I've still got my roscoe an' I got the drop on ya. Grab some sky or you'll be pushin' up daisies. Nobody's blowin' the whistle on my baby. Cookie, pull the phone outta the wall.

COOKIE: Aw Daddy, it's so hard to get service from Ma Bell.

GASPARI: *(Genuinely frightened)* What d'you think yer doin', Shooter?

SHOOTER: Shooter it is, pally-o. Two of us are one too many for this crew.

PEACHES: *(To SHOOTER with more irritation than concern)* Stop the horseplay an' gimmee the gun.

SHOOTER: *(Turning the gun on unperterbed PEACHES)* Who're you, baby?

PEACHES: I'm your granddaughter.

SHOOTER: Don't play on my sentiments.

TRIXIE: *(Casually)* Shooter, please spare my father.

SHOOTER: What's it worth t'you?

TRIXIE: I'll get you a beer.

GASPARI: *(Genuinely fearful)* That's all I'm worth??? A beer!

SHOOTER: *(To TRIXIE)* No dice, baby. I just put five notches on this heater. They can only hang you once.

GASPARI: *(Into the phone)* HELP! I'M ABOUT TO BE SHOT!!! Dammit, I've *been* on hold! *(He slams the phone onto the receiver)*

SHOOTER: Get ready t'meet yer maker.

GASPARI: *(Terrified)* Shooter, I didn't mean all those things I said about—

(DENISE screams. SHOOTER pulls the trigger. Click!)

SHOOTER: *(In unison with the click)* BANG!

(GASPARI collapses with a moan. Only DENISE seems particularly concerned. After a long moment, GASPARI checks his chest as SHOOTER blows imaginary smoke through the barrel. Determining that he's O K, GASPARI rushes off to the bathroom shouting....)

GASPARI: Yooooo!!!

TRIXIE: *(To SHOOTER)* Very funny.

SHOOTER: I'd never shoot a member of the family. *(Pointing at FRANJO)* Unless he went over t'New Quakers.

PEACHES: You could've killed someone, today.

SHOOTER: Only if I wanted to. Hell, in the old days it was an honor t'get wounded. It meant you were a threat.

TRIXIE: You're a threat to my sanity. You all are. The Mummers are drivin' me bats.

PEACHES: Well, in that case Trix, what's gotta be done, gotta be done. I'll hafta take it upon myself t'be the first mummer of my sex.

COOKIE: What's alla this talk about sex?

FRANJO: Atta girl, Mom.

PEACHES: Unless *you* wanna march, Momma.

COOKIE: *(Shaking her head)* A tradition's a tradition. Right or wrong.

TRIXIE: One small step for womanhood, one giant step towards lunacy.

(FRANJO and DENISE are at the bar exchanging small intimacies.)

PEACHES: Help me with this. *(Cookie and Trixie help her to don Gaspari's cape)* I'm doin' this for you, Trix. I know how much the parade disturbed ya.

TRIXIE: *(Smiles)* You're doin' it for yourself, Mom.

PEACHES: Well, whatever...Whatever you think is a step forward gotta be taken.

TRIXIE: I gotta funny feelin' you're gonna be worse than the guys.

PEACHES: Better!

(TRIXIE puts on string band music. FRANJO and DENISE, SPIKE and PEACHES, SHOOTER and COOKIE strut as partners. COOKIE will drift to the window to look

out leaving SHOOTER *to dance—fittingly—on his own.* GASPARI *emerges from the bathroom too drunk and despondent to notice his wife. He heads for a refill.)*

PEACHES: C'mon, Gas.

GASPARI: Through! I've had it.

PEACHES: Ya can't quit now. It's a brand new parade. In a couple of years, it'll be status. An' plenty of lawsuits when we break the rules. Lotsa business.

GASPARI: Don't care about business. Don't care about nothin'.

PEACHES: O K, if ya won't strut for business, will ya strut for me?

(He looks up and is enthralled by her appearance. PEACHES *continues...)*

PEACHES: Alla these years I served the Mummers. Will ya strut with me in next year's parade?

GASPARI: *(Readily reconsidering)* For you...anything, Babe.

(He crosses, kisses his wife and they start to strut. FRANJO *and* DENISE— *unnoticed by the others—are doing a semi-erotic strut.)*

(SPIKE moves away to allow GASPARI *to strut with* PEACHES. *Then* SPIKE *turns happily to dance with his wife. He sees her at the window. He turns solemn.* TRIXIE *sees what has transpired as* SPIKE *crosses to* COOKIE. *He says something to his wife. He attempts to explain the sad fact to her. But he can't be heard over the music. Nonetheless,* COOKIE *isn't listening as he shakes his head and tries to reason with her. She is oblivious.* SPIKE *turns away with profound sadness. He and* TRIXIE *engage each other visually, since she has known what's transpiring. He bows his head, tears welling up in his eyes.* TRIXIE *embraces him as the revelry by the others continues.)*

(The lights dim slowly almost to dark as the music fades. This gives DENISE *time—and shadow—to emerge in a spot, as at the top of the play. Her coat's been removed, and her afro. She again addresses the audience.)*

DENISE: I wasn't fired from W C A U. Mainly because my six o'clock, on-camera revelry was overshadowed by anchorman Dennis Perkins' at eleven. He also covered the parade—*and* some ensuing parties—then threw up...on-camera. I called the station president the next day and suggested that if he was firing this little pickenenny then he'd better fire the white anchorman. Before I could mention N A A C P he had already rehired me. The public loved my performance and sympathized with my plight as the wronged woman...doubly so. I was in Philly at just the right time. As long as I wasn't an Angela Davis clone... As long as my hair was a fashion statement, I was acceptable. Respectable, even. A breath of fresh air. Though an inebriated one for the only time in my life.

I continued to play T V Topsy, though I was raging inside. The deaths of

Martin, Medgar and Malcolm were a part of my growing up. And yes,
the Kennedy boys. I'd often ask myself, "What if they had all lived?
What if even some of them had?"

So, I took advantage. I focused. I began to make friends...build a life...
a career. I stayed in touch with Trixie. I stayed in special touch with Franjo.
I got him a job as an apprentice at the station. He became obsessive just as
he had with the mummers. By next year, he had no great desire to strut.
He covered the parade for us as a cameraman. Peaches never did become
the first mummerette because Cookie was sent away again. And never
came out. Shooter passed on. The neighborhood changed and Spike sold
the bar to an African-American. With no regret, Trixie told me. Just a sense
of resignation that the O'Rourke's day had passed. Others were taking over.
Then Spike too, passed. After living all alone.

Gaspari became particularly proud of Franjo. He credited me with setting
his son...*straight*. Well...setting his son on a viable career path. Mary Jane
Ciparelli was not for Franjo. She merely became his convenient friend...
his situational date. On Franjo's twenty-first birthday, Peaches and Gaspari
invited him and Mary Jane, Trixie and her new boyfriend and me and
my fiance to the country club. Franjo had gotten a raise and was about to
become a head cameraman. The family glowed with pride. And I glowed
with them. Gaspari later received a reprimand from his club for having
invited me. He walked into their next meeting and tore up his membership.
Then Franjo was proud of Gaspari. And so was I. But in 1985, Franjo became
ill ...due to his life style. I had known. Trixie had known. We suspected
that Peaches had known. But Gaspari hadn't a clue. He was shocked and
embarrassed and he denied Franjo in his greatest need. He diminished
himself. Despite pleas from his wife and daughter, Gaspari was
unforgiving. Until the very end. And then it was too late.

(Spot up on TRIXIE—*older now—dressed in a fur coat and dialing a cell phone.)*

(Spot up on PEACHES, *home in a housedress. She's hardly a shadow of* COOKIE *but
there's a certain agedness that reflects her mother.)*

DENISE: *(Continuing under the action)* Trixie married well and raises two
hellions of her own. She asked me to be godmother to Alice. But I, well...
I declined. I'd been married twice, divorced each time. No kids. *No time.* I'm
on a career course in New York, now. A media, corporate vice-president. I
wouldn't make a very good godmother. So much for assimilation.

(PEACHES *answers the phone [that the audience never hears ring]. A third spot
comes up on grey-haired* GASPARI, *sitting in an armchair reading a paper. He takes
off his glasses when he determines who is talking (silently) to his wife. He would
desperately love to talk to his daughter. He crosses to* PEACHES.)

DENISE: The mummers were long ago. A germinal point on my rise up the
ladder. I can't say it was a better time then. Certainly not more innocent.

Women strut down Broad Street now. African-Americans could if they so choose. But we have our own parade, dearly-earned...hard-won. I connected with the mummers for a brief, fleeting moment. But the chasm was too wide. All things considered, it was a moment I don't regret. And won't forget.

(PEACHES *slowly extends the phone to* GASPARI. *He takes it and utters...*)

GASPARI: Angela...my angel.

(TRIXIE *hangs up. Her light goes out.* GASPARI *is crushed.* PEACHES *stands still, facing front...expressionless.* GASPARI—*behind her—lays his head on her shoulder...and weeps.*)

(*All lights fade out.*)

END OF PLAY

DANCIN' TO
CALLIOPE

ACKNOWLEDGMENTS

For support with the development of DANCIN' TO CALLIOPE, thanks to New Dramatists as well as The Festival of Southern Theater, Department of Theater Arts, University of Mississippi, Oxford MS, Scott McCoy, Artistic Director and Kelly Brainard, Michael Campbell, Valerie Galloway, Victor Lazarow and Mark Waterman; EARPLAY and Daniel Freudenberger, John Lithgow, Christine Baranski and June Gable.

DANCIN' TO CALLIOPE was the winner of The Festival of Southern Theater Playwriting Award

for the memory of Nomi Mitty and for Jo

CHARACTERS & SETTING

RICKY RUANE, *handsome, late twenties. None too bright. An ex-con who has yet to be "with it" (accepted in carnival life). Breaks the rules. Enacts the "Half and Half" (man and woman) in the ten-in-one (sideshow).*

SHAUNELLE, *his carny "wife". Mid-to-upper thirties. The mermaid in the ten-in-one. Attractive, street-smart, born into carnival life. Formerly a kootchie dancer (stripper). Her incurable romanticism is both attractive and destructive.*

LU RAE, SHAUNELLE's *eighteen-year-old step-daughter. A kootchie dancer. Her fresh beauty is a poignant contrast to her sordid profession. But she loves the life.*

BARNEY HARRELSON, *older. The owner/manager of the carnival. Sweet on* SHAUNELLE *(which she isn't above exploiting).*

BEAZLEY, *a good ole boy, rural sheriff.*

Time: the 1990s

Place: on the road with the very last old-time carnival.

ACT ONE

(Before the lights come up—and over the calliope music—we hear a carnival barker "pitching" the freak show over a mike. The lights will rise slowly with the spiel.)

BARNEY: Now, ladies and gentlemen, we got Pinky The Pincushion...Gloria The Gorilla Lady...Connie The Contortionist...Lucy, The Bearded Lady... The Baron And His Little People...Fuego, The Fire Eater...Zenobia, The Snake Lady...Treetop Tommy The Giant...Illustrated Ike...Prince Electro, who you may remember as The Sultan of Sabres until he started swallowin' neon tubes... Oh, I could go on and on...

(The lights are full-up now, backstage of the freak show. RICKY is waiting glumly to go on.)

(The opening scene is theoretically played in front of the stage curtain [which is stenciled in reverse "Freaks Of The World"]. Only RICKY, The Half And Half will occupy this area at the outset. He wears gym shorts. He wears one man's shoe and a woman's high heel shoe. Thus when he walks, he wobbles. He wears a woman's stocking and a man's sock. If need be, one leg is shaven. He wears an old fashioned "strong man's" skin-tight shirt with one shoulder strap only. The exposed side of his chest is unshaven. The shirt strap covers the female side of his chest which of course, has a makeshift "breast" underneath. He wears a half-beard on one side and a long half-wig on the clean-shaven [female] side of his face. He wears conspicuous make-up on his female side.)

(On the other side of the curtain the freak show is in progress. With back-lighting, we can vaguely see the proceedings through the stenciled curtain. We should make out the figures of a seated woman [SHAUNELLE] dressed in a halter and a tailfin and a barker with a cane [BARNEY]. They play with their backs to us and facing the [imagined] carnival audience. Thus we view everything from backstage.)

(The calliope music could be "The Loveliest Night of The Year" [for the sake of irony] and we should hear thrill rides and "atmosphere" faintly in the background.)

RICKY: *(Calling angrily to BARNEY)* Why don't ya tell 'im about *me*, Barney?

BARNEY: *(Turning to RICKY, then the carnival audience)* An' for those of you with a strong stomach, you'll meet the most pitiful...pathetic...disgustin'...

(RICKY gives BARNEY the finger.)

SHAUNELLE: 'Nuff said, Barney. These folks come to see me. Huh, boys?

(Cheers from the customers)

BARNEY: *(Focusing on* SHAUNELLE*)* And isn't she a sight, folks? A truly unique and aquatic vision. Unrivalled on land or sea. Shaunelle The Mermaid. "The Star of The Sea". Isn't she a beautiful girl, folks?

VOICE I: *(Off)* Girl??? She ain't no girl.

BARNEY: Well, lady then.

VOICE II: *(Off)* She ain't no lady neither.

(Guffaws, stirring from the patrons)

SHAUNELLE: Neither's your mother.

(Hoots, whistles...)

VOICE I: *(Off)* She's a fish.

SHAUNELLE: So's your wife.

(More hoots)

BARNEY: Well, whatever she is she's one of nature's true mysteries. This is just the way we found her offa coral reef close by the Pacific Island of Olakalakamookoo.

RICKY: *(To himself)* She ain't never been west of Las Vegas.

VOICE I: *(Off)* Hey, Barker Man, didn't we see her inna kootchie show last year?

VOICE II: *(Off)* An' a whole lotta years before that?

(Laughter and shouts of agreement)

BARNEY: Naw, naw, we just fished 'er outta the drink.

SHAUNELLE: How could you see me kootchie? I got no legs. Musta been a beautiful human lady.

VOICE II: *(Off)* How do you do it?

SHAUNELLE: "It"???

VOICE II: *(Off)* How d'you make love?

RICKY: *(Angrily to himself)* Now it starts, dammit!

SHAUNELLE: Beautifully!

(Whoops and cheers)

BARNEY: *(Quietly to* SHAUNELLE*)* That's enough, Shaun.

VOICE II: *(Off)* Well, maybe I'd like to see about that.

*(*RICKY *boils as the cheers continue.)*

SHAUNELLE: You make it with me and you'll never go back to your wife.

BARNEY: Dammit, Shaun!!! Why you always incitin'???

SHAUNELLE: *Ex*citin', Barney? I just can't help it.

VOICE I: *(Off)* Well, I ain't married so I got nothin' t'lose. I'm comin' up fer a piece a'mermaid.

BARNEY: *(Threatening the potential intruder)* Don't you climb up here, boy!

SHAUNELLE: RICKY...RICKY!!!

RICKY: *(About to enter the "runway" through the curtain)* Here I come, baby!

(But BARNEY *anticipates* RICKY'*s entrance, separates the curtain and bops* RICKY *with his cane as he's about to hobble onto the ten-in-one stage [runway].* RICKY *falls back.)*

BARNEY: You wait your turn, stupid. You're supposed to be a surprise. *(Retreating back to* SHAUNELLE *and the trouble)* That's it, folks! Let's have a little hand for Shaunelle, The Star of The Sea. *(Sotto voce to* SHAUNELLE*)* Let's get outta here.

(Weak applause, a few scattered boos and a "Take it off!" SHAUNELLE *gives the audience the finger as* BARNEY *picks her up in his arms and comes through the curtain separation. He hands her to* RICKY.*)*

SHAUNELLE: "Little hand" is right.

BARNEY: Deadbeats. *(To* RICKY*)* Don't drop Shaunelle, here. She's my prize possession.

SHAUNELLE: I ain't nobody's possession.

BARNEY: *One a'these days you're gonna go too far, boy.*

*(*BARNEY *retreats behind the curtain again, to continue the show.* RICKY *carries* SHAUNELLE *to a bench and puts her down gently.)*

SHAUNELLE: Now ya done it, Rick. It's "humiliation time".

BARNEY: *(Back on the other side of the curtain and addressing the—theoretically upstage—carnival audience)* Step right up, folks. This ten-in-one tent— small as it is—holds the saddest, most pitiful array of humanity on the face of the earth.

RICKY: *(To* SHAUNELLE*)* Barney's right at the top of the pitiful heap.

SHAUNELLE: You mean the bottom. But that attitude will get you nowheres.

*(*RICKY *will help* SHAUNELLE *off with her tailfin [under which she wears tights]. He'll massage her legs tenderly, then prepare to go on, reluctantly.)*

RICKY: We are nowheres. Boonesville Junction, U S of A.

BARNEY: *(To the carnival audience)* And as a bit of a bonus to you good folks, I'm gonna innerduce you to the freakiest of the freaks.

RICKY: Why's he always pick on me?

BARNEY: I'm tryna do justice to his description, folks.

SHAUNELLE: *(To* RICKY*)* You know he's tryna get you to quit.

BARNEY:Ridiculous...absurd...grotesque...distorted...gruesome...hideous... ridiculous—

RICKY: *(Shouting)* YOU ALREADY SAID "RIDICULOUS"!

BARNEY: *(Calling back)* Can't say it enough in your case.

SHAUNELLE: You quit, then Barney figures he's in the driver's seat with me.

BARNEY: Let's give this poor fella...oops, did I say "fella"? Well, that's only half right. The other half's of the distaff persuasion.

VOICE I: *(Off)* Wujoo say?

BARNEY: Why, the other half's of the feminine gender.

(Laughter...hoots as RICKY *puts on his robe and approaches the split in the curtain. He hesitates, turns to* SHAUNELLE. *She urges him on.)*

BARNEY: Now, let's have a hand for this poor monstrosity.

*(*RICKY *extends his hand to* SHAUNELLE, *lovingly. She crosses and kisses him gently.)*

BARNEY: *(Louder)* ...for this poor monstrosity! *(Sticking his head through the curtain)* Get yer ass out here, boy!

*(*RICKY *gives him a look and then kisses* SHAUNELLE *with a reciprocated passion.)*

BARNEY: *(Hysterically at the pair)* Sabotage! Sabotage! Sabotage!

*(*BARNEY *withdraws in a feverish state.* RICKY *releases* SHAUNELLE *and proceeds through the curtain.* SHAUNELLE *puts on a robe. We can see* RICKY *remove his robe through the curtain. Laughter breaks out... cat-calls... whistles. She stands still, quietly suffering with* RICKY *as the derision builds to a crescendo. The calliope comes up as the lights ...)*

(Fadeout)

(End of Scene One)

Scene Two

(The curtain has been flown. The "in one" bench has been removed. The stage is dominated by a trailer—downstage wall removed—with playing space in front. The living/dining room area, kitchen and bedroom are in view.)

(Doors lead off to the bedroom and closet. The trailer is a mess with robes and kootchie outfits strewn about. Movie posters cover the walls. Dishes fill the sink. Knicknacks picked up throughout the country are in evidence, e.g. Olympic pennant, souvenirs from Disneyland, New Orleans, etc. There is a map of the U S on the back wall and a route is traced in bold red. One point in mid-America about an inch from where the red trail stops is a huge dark "X".)

(Calliope music plays in the background throughout.)

(Lights up on SHAUNELLE and RICKY as they enter downstage of the trailer in no particular hurry to get home. RICKY still lurches from the two different shoes. She wears her robe, his is slung over his shoulder. He carries his half-beard and half-wig and SHAUNELLE's tailfin. RICKY stops and fingers his single breast.)

RICKY: This is one helluva way to make a livin'.

(RICKY lowers the single shoulder strap of his costume and starts to peel off the adhesive-attached "falsie" with caution. SHAUNELLE reaches over and rips it off. RICKY howls.)

SHAUNELLE: They mock me, too!

RICKY: Not like they mock me. They want me to drop my drawers. Wanna see whats down south. You don't have that problem. You don't wear no drawers since you don't have legs. But me...hell, they get their moneys worth when they take a gander at me. But that ain't enough for 'em.

SHAUNELLE: Well, ya gotta admit Rick, you're not exactly the boy next door.

RICKY: The girl, neither!

SHAUNELLE: Look, I tole ya what to say. Tell 'em that ya got-

RICKY: Yeah... yeah... I tell 'em that.

(She exercises her stiff legs. RICKY sits and removes his shoes.)

RICKY: That I got one set a'male and one set a'female. That just turns 'em on. Then I gotta explain about the risk of me gettin' arrested for obscenity. They just starts yellin' about the girls flashin' down the midway. An' I sez that I ain't a girl, an' it's against the law for a half 'n half to expose himself... herself...itself...whatever. Geez, I do suffer from one a'them identity crises. So, I just cuss 'em a bit an' I head off with you an' your fishtail to our little home on wheels.

SHAUNELLE: God bless our little home on wheels.

RICKY: Amen t'that.

SHAUNELLE: An' it ain't a fish tale. A fish tale's a cock 'n bull story.

RICKY: Mermaid's tail. Mermaid's tale! Geez, you're startin' to believe you're real.

SHAUNELLE: At least you're workin'. This time last year you were inna penitentiary an—

RICKY: I don't wanna hear about this time last year.

SHAUNELLE: Then stop yer bitchin'. We gotta whole evenin' ahead of us.

RICKY: We oughtta get a union. These hours stink. Kootchies're lucky.

SHAUNELLE: What???

RICKY: Cause there ain't no call for kootchie in the daytime. Good ole boys're drivin' their rigs...punchin' their cows...tendin' their bars. LuRae's got it knocked.

SHAUNELLE: Don't ever tell a kootchie she's got it knocked.

RICKY: G'wan, she's happy as a pig in shit.

SHAUNELLE: Kootchyin's a rough racket. It's humiliatin', some of the things they call you.

RICKY: Nothin' they'd call LuRae would bother me.

SHAUNELLE: She says she's happy 'cause she don't know no better. She's light years younger than those other girls an' really pretty t'boot. Just like I was at eighteen. A big turd in a small cesspool. She'll learn in a hurry.

RICKY: I dunno. Cherry Vanillas been kootchyin' for sixteen years an' she savors it more each day.

SHAUNELLE: Cherry's a low achiever. An' that's speakin' highly of her.

(She sits. RICKY massages her shoulders. When he's through, they exchange places.)

RICKY: Cherry's just a little slow, that's all.

SHAUNELLE: Ricky, *you're* a little slow but next to Cherry, you're operatin' in overdrive. Sixteen years ago, Barney tole Cherry that alla big movie stars started this way. An he tells her that every time he wants her to re-sign. Cherry figures her next gig will be Scarlett O'Hara in the remake of *Gone With The Wind*. An while I'm on the subject, don't you get caught talkin' t'Cherry. The Baron is a jealous little bastard.

RICKY: The Baron??? You think I'm afraid of a pipsqueak midget?

SHAUNELLE: Not midget! Dwarf! Y'know how he screams about "Dwarf Entitlement". How dwarfhood's beautiful.

RICKY: Damn, everybody's somebody, nowadays. Whatever he is, he can't even reach me to hit me.

SHAUNELLE: He can reach high enough with his knife to give you a sex change. Then you'll be outta work as a Half 'n Half. *(Exasperated beat)* When are you gonna learn the ropes? You're still not "with it", buddy-boy. The others won't acknowledge you. You won't learn carny language. You're unacceptable.

RICKY: What's the difference? We wont be carnies much longer, anyway.

SHAUNELLE: We wont be alive much longer but we wanna go out on *our* terms. Not anyone else's. You just stay away from Cherry.

RICKY: Damn, Shaunelle. Would I be interested in her when I got you? You're still the prettiest woman on the whole midway.

SHAUNELLE: Whataya mean, *still*? I've yet to hit my peak.

RICKY: Right. That's what I meant to say. I'd give my body to science before I'd give it to Cherry.

SHAUNELLE: An' yer showin' precious little thanks t'Barney Harrelson.

RICKY: Fer what? The piddlin' amount of dough-re-me he pays?

SHAUNELLE: Well, he's goin' broke. There's no more call for carnival. It's politically incorrect.

RICKY: That ain't it. You can see freaks onna T V talk shows. An' you can see flesh onna cable. Morals ain't improvin'. Folks're just too lazy to leave the house.

SHAUNELLE: We're the last *true* carnival. Barneys keepin' a great American tradition alive. An' if Barney didn't go to bat for ya, ya wouldn'ta been paroled.

RICKY: He did it for you, not me. He'll do anythin' for you.

SHAUNELLE: Whatever. You're free now, ain't ya?

RICKY: Of sorts.

SHAUNELLE: Of sorts?

RICKY: Kinda.

SHAUNELLE: Kinda?

RICKY: Yeah.

SHAUNELLE: Yeah?
What's 'at supposed t'mean?

RICKY: It means that when I was inna slammer, I was a heavy honcho. Y'know...legit. Recognized. "With it" as carnies say. Armed robbery! The Big Leagues. The day I walked inta the cellblock...instant respect.

SHAUNELLE: They woulda respected you more if ya hadn't got caught.

RICKY: If I hadn't got caught, they never woulda knowed me.

(They enter the trailer. She flops on the open foldaway.)

RICKY: Here, even the freaks look down on me. Even The Baron's Little People. That don't boost yer ego none, t'havin' midgets look down on ya.

SHAUNELLE: It's nothin' personal. It's just that they're naturals and we're fakes. The legitimate product is always more valuable than the imitation. Like antiques.

RICKY: What's antiques gotta do with it?

SHAUNELLE: Forget it. It'd just go over your head.

RICKY: When you get right down to it, we ain't even self-made freaks. I mean, Illustrated Ike... he's self-made. And Fuego The Fire Eater. Connie The Contortionist. They worked years on their gimmick. But we ain't natural *or* self-made. We're just phonies dressed up in costume an' make-up. Phonies, through an' through. *(Beat)* How does the fire eater do that?

SHAUNELLE: You know self-mades never tell. All I know is that he's developed a resistance to pain.

RICKY: Wish we had the hang of that.

SHAUNELLE: He says the pain is in the mind. Actually, he said, " The fire's in the mind." That's just how he put it.

RICKY: He also said, "Don't breathe in."

(He starts removing the make-up. She opens the refrigerator.)

SHAUNELLE: Wish we had some coke.

RICKY: We can't afford it.

SHAUNELLE: We can afford the drinkin' kind. *(She slams, angrily)*

RICKY: Soda don't ease the pain.

(She converts the foldaway then starts to dress. RICKY will dress when he's removed his make-up. When SHAUNELLE's finished, she'll collect all the clothes strewn about and throw them in a heap in the closet. She'll deposit dirty dishes in the sink with the others and then she'll drape a towel over the heap. RICKY pitches in by throwing any papers, garbage, trash out the door. She'll use air freshener as a finishing touch. All of this is done under conversation and the business should take us to "the ritual".)

SHAUNELLE: Look at it this way. At least we can pass in the straight world. The freaks can't. The self-mades won't. We can mingle with the marks when we hafta.

RICKY: But we ain't livin' with the marks. We're livin' with the freaks.

SHAUNELLE: It wasn't carnies put you inna can. It was marks. Carnies wouldn't turn someone over to the law. Not even you.

RICKY: Well, only God can help us with this caper you're plannin'. I almost wish you didn't get Barney t'spring me. I go three years protectin' my manhood from perverts as well as deviates. I get out of the hoosegow, and Barney slaps a falsie on me.

SHAUNELLE: He needed a Half 'n Half. Everybody knows you're my man. That makes you all man. So ya wish you were back in the cooler, huh?

RICKY: Well, makin' license plates was less humiliatin'. *(Caressing her warmly)* I ain't complainin', though. I'm ready to die for you, ain't I? You waited for me while I was up the river.

SHAUNELLE: My choice.

RICKY: Still, Barney coulda used me some other way. I woulda got my body tattooed.

SHAUNELLE: What would Barney do with Illustrated Ike?

RICKY: I coulda handled snakes.

SHAUNELLE: Only women handle snakes. He says it's sexier.

RICKY: Sexy? What's sexy about a snake? Barney's weird. He wanted me to be a Wild Man of Borneo.

SHAUNELLE: I vetoed that.

RICKY: I coulda handled it. From what I hear, all they do is yell and scream and jump around. Hell, I do that when I drink rot gut with the ride boys.

SHAUNELLE: What happens when some wise-ass mark throws a live chicken or a rat into the pit?

RICKY: I ain't afraid of rats. Had 'em in jail. My cellblock had a rat as a mascot 'til the guard blew its head off... Insensitive bastard.

SHAUNELLE: Wild Men are geeks, dummy. Why d'you think they carry on so? Anybody bites the heads offa livin' creatures has gotta be a bit flakey.

RICKY: *(Appalled)* They *really* do that? I figgered it was all trickery.

SHAUNELLE: I mean *fried* chicken don't agree with me but at least it's dead.

RICKY: I thought all that Wild Men ate was cigarettes. I could handle that. I mean, I chew tobacco.

SHAUNELLE: I met a geek one time said she'd never do cigarettes. Said nobody ever got cancer bitin' the heads offa chickens.

RICKY: How can "she" be a Wild Man of Borneo?

SHAUNELLE: They called her a "wild woman".

(RICKY nods, assured as she continues...)

SHAUNELLE: Speakin' of wild women, where the hell is Lu Rae? She's gotta work tonight.

RICKY: Relax, it's a long trip.

SHAUNELLE: Maybe the sheriff done to her what he done t'me.

RICKY: Nah, she may only be a kid but no guy'll ever outfox 'er.

SHAUNELLE: Yeah, well no guy's ever put a thirty-eight t'her head yet neither. If Beazley's still sheriff there... *(Pointing to the "X" on the map she continues...)* ...he can do anythin' he wants. Long as he does it to outsiders.

RICKY: Hey, maybe he done it to a local girl an' got blowed away by her kin.

SHAUNELLE:Geez, iffn somebody croaked him, then alla our plans will be a waste.

RICKY: *(Brightly)* An' alla our problems will be solved.

SHAUNELLE: Not so. I'll be cheated outta my vengeance.

RICKY: But we'd be able to live. He's dead. We're alive. We win.

(SHAUNELLE snarls at him. Defensively, he continues...)

RICKY: I'm sorry. I was just tryna think optimistic.

SHAUNELLE: Well, perish that sorta thinkin'.

(She starts a stylized dance to the calliope music. His back is to her.)

RICKY: You dancin'?

SHAUNELLE: Yeah, what of it?

RICKY: You're rockin' the boat.

SHAUNELLE: Not rockin' the boat. Swayin' the trailer. I was raised up on calliope. It's in my blood.

RICKY: Ya tole me... ya tole me.

SHAUNELLE: Yer jealous, Ricky Roo. Alla that country 'n western corroded yer taste for pure music.

RICKY: Calliope's arright. In small doses. It keeps me awake at night.

SHAUNELLE: See, it's cast a spell over ya. We even got married t'calliope. Like true carnies should.

RICKY: *(Unimpressed)* Yeah, goin round 'n round onna merry-go-round.

SHAUNELLE: Carousel!!! Dammit Ricky, merry-go-round is what *they* call it, not us. Nobody trusts you cause you talk like a mark.

RICKY: O K, O K, carousel. Goin' round in circles, gettin' nowheres. That's carny, arright. An' how legit's our weddin', Shaunelle? Barney's no preacher.

SHAUNELLE: The carny boss conducts everythin'. Weddin's...bust-ups...births...burials... the works.

RICKY: The law don't recanize a carny weddin'.

SHAUNELLE: So what? We don't recanize the law.

RICKY: Well, let's just wash our hands of the law an' abandon your Beazley brainstorm. I can't see no way outta this predicament. No escape...no way.

SHAUNELLE: We'll escape t' eternity. T' paradise. Mark my words.

RICKY: We won't be around t' mark your words.

SHAUNELLE: There's a slim chance we can call this off. Iff'n I get the word.

RICKY: The word from who?

SHAUNELLE: From God.

RICKY: When he calls, tell 'em he's been sleepin' onna job lately.

SHAUNELLE: *(Grimly)* You backin' down?

RICKY: I din't say I was backin' down. It wouldn't be fair t' you.

SHAUNELLE: It wouldn't be fair t' either one a'us.

RICKY: Well, speakin' for myself—

SHAUNELLE: *(As she dances into the bedroom...)* My momma tole me I didn't *take* my first step. I *danced* it. I started out in life dancin' to calliope. That's when she knew I'd be a part of this life for alla my life. You wouldn't understand that, Ricky, bein' a "first a'May-er". Just along for a little excitement... a little dough durin' the peak months. An opportunist.

RICKY: So I thought.

SHAUNELLE: It was written all over your face. Written all over your pretty teeth, even. *(Prying his jaw open and examining his teeth)* Amazin'! No rot. No gaps. There's no man hereabouts got teeth so perfect. The ride boys even take pride in their bad ivory. They chip 'em out with a hammer. Makes 'em feel approved. But they're still at the ass-end of the carney dung heap.

RICKY: "Ree-a-zide, bee-a-zoy." Izzat correct? Izzat "ride boy" in carney lingo?

SHAUNELLE: Anybody can learn one syllable words.

RICKY: It's a start. An' "ride boys" is two syllables.

SHAUNELLE: It's two WORDS! Geez!
Yeah, soon's I spotted your pearly whites, I says t'myself, "This guy's different".

RICKY: I mighta joined up as a "first a'May-er" but soon's I seen you, I knew I wanted t'stay.

SHAUNELLE: But ya didn't.

RICKY: I pulled that stick-up so's I could treat you in style. Only I got nabbed an' off t'the pokey. Don't ever forget that.

SHAUNELLE: Lord, how could I? Kootchyin' my ass across the states an' inta the provinces. Waitin' fer you t'get sprung.

RICKY: I just figgered quick money was the way to yer heart. Like with most girls. I figure a heist would get you t'notice me.

SHAUNELLE: I tole ya, I noticed ya.

RICKY: (Irritably) Ya noticed my teeth. I'm more'n teeth. You didn't really care fer me 'til I pulled that caper just fer you.

SHAUNELLE: Even if it was stupid, it was a romantic gesture. I felt like Bonnie might've felt for Clyde.

(RICKY nods, impressed with the analogy. SHAUNELLE continues...)

SHAUNELLE: Truly impressed.

RICKY: Then I'm glad I done it, inna long run.

SHAUNELLE: Hardly a long run. They caught ya after three blocks.

RICKY: I ran outta gas.

SHAUNELLE: You shoulda gassed up beforehand.

RICKY: I can't remember everythin' when it's crunch time. Anyway, the gesture was what counted.

SHAUNELLE: I know. But I didn't ask you stick up that car wash. On a rainy day, no less. We were doin okey-dokey. Me kootchyin' an' you runnin' the hanky-pank. But ya hadda get greedy.

RICKY: I wanted t' load ya down with furs an' finery. Trips t'Europe. Fast cars.

SHAUNELLE: Then ya shoulda robbed a bank! Yer gonna flop, flop big. Anyway, I never needed those things. Ya don't miss what you never had. God knows, my first husband never gave me nothin' of that sort.

RICKY: I wanted t' surprise you.

SHAUNELLE: Ya did that arright. The only thing ya coulda done dumber was rob the carnival, itself.

RICKY: Fact is, I thought on that a bit but I abandoned the idea.

SHAUNELLE: No, Rick. Ideas abandon you.

(The calliope stops. She stops dancing.)

RICKY: Dinner, soon.

SHAUNELLE: An' no Lu Rae in sight.

RICKY: *(Surveying the trailer)* I must say, Shaun. You are one top-notch housekeeper. *(Beat)* Wanna practice?

SHAUNELLE: Practice?

RICKY: Our little...uh, what'd you call it?

SHAUNELLE: "Ritual."

RICKY: Yeah.

SHAUNELLE: Somehow, it seems t' me you don't practice a ritual. You rehearse a ritual. I mean like, if it's a contest...y' know, like a sport or somethin'...then ya practice. But if it's a ritual...well then ya rehearse. I mean like ya rehearse for playactin', for instance. But ya practice football. Dig it?

RICKY: Suppose so. *(Beat)* What about a ceremony? Is that a result of practice?

SHAUNELLE: I would say...I would say, a ceremony's the result of rehearsal.

RICKY: *(Befuddled by now)* S'pose so.

SHAUNELLE: I'm firmly convinced.

RICKY: What about a pageant?

SHAUNELLE: *(Ponders)* Rehearsal,... I think. Could be either, though. If there's music.

RICKY: What about a drink?

SHAUNELLE: Oh, yeah. Our little happy hour libation. *(She removes two cheap beers from the refrigerator.)* Rehearsal. I've determined it's a rehearsal.

RICKY: S'pose so. *(Beat)* Say, what is a pageant? Officially speakin'?

SHAUNELLE: Who's talkin' about a pageant? Let's rehearse the ritual.

RICKY: Right. *(He crosses to a drawer and takes out a pistol.)*

SHAUNELLE: Ya still don't have it down yet. After alla the times we been through this.

RICKY: You're always changin' things. Changes confuse me.

SHAUNELLE: Well, concentrate. We only get one crack at this.

RICKY: I still say we oughtta torture 'im.

SHAUNELLE: Torture's inhumane.

RICKY: Boy, are you naive. Nyyyy-eeeeeve!

SHAUNELLE: He didn't torture me.

RICKY: *(Incredulously)* You said he forced hisself on you...sexially. At gunpoint. That's not torture?

SHAUNELLE: It'll be payback when he looks down my gun barrel.

RICKY: We oughtta tie 'im up an' pour sugar over his body. Then watch the insects eat 'im alive.

SHAUNELLE: It was more mental than physical.

RICKY: We could take 'im to a desert, tie 'im down, slap a slab a'rabbit meat on his crotch for the vultures. Then prop his eyes open with matchsticks. The sun'll burn out his irises.

SHAUNELLE: There's no desert hereabouts.

RICKY: You gotta point. I'm glad you protect me from my own ideas. *(Afterthought)* How 'bout if we hang 'im upsidedown an' poke a hole in his head. White he bleeds t' death we could use a cattle prod on his genitals. Then we rub wintergreen over his body while we pour acid a bit at a time all over his—

SHAUNELLE: What are you babblin' about???

RICKY: I thought you had an axe to grind! *(Beat)* Say, there's another hundinger idea. I'll get an axe—

SHAUNELLE: How come when it comes to atrocities, your imagination suddenly springs to life?

RICKY: Y'know, I hear about things. Here...there. Jail. Jail's a pretty good source.

SHAUNELLE: They torture you in jail?

RICKY: Not me. I was a model con. I may have been a criminal but I wasn't very dedicated.

SHAUNELLE: No torture! I just wanna zap him face-front so's I can see the expression on his face when I fire. O K, Let's cut the diddley-shittin' around. Gimmee the piece.

(He hands her the gun. Both take positions a couple of feet apart and facing an imaginary Beazley.)

SHAUNELLE: Ready?

RICKY: Couldn't be more so.

SHAUNELLE: A simple "yes" or "no" will do.

RICKY: Right.

SHAUNELLE: Well, are you ready???

RICKY: Whataya think, I'm waitin' for a bus?

SHAUNELLE: O K, roll 'em.

RICKY: Roll 'im? I thought we were gonna shoot 'im.

SHAUNELLE: It's an expression. It means, "Get started".

RICKY: I know it's an expression. But iffn we're gonna roll 'im, we oughtta shoot im first. It'd be a lot easier.

SHAUNELLE: It's movie lingo.

RICKY: This ain't no movie.

SHAUNELLE: You can say that again.

RICKY: Why? You need a reminder?
Movies are fulla fantasy an' such.

SHAUNELLE: What's wrong with fantasy? I savor fantasy.

RICKY: This here's ordinary, everyday life. An' don't throw me yer cutesy expressions like "roll 'im".

SHAUNELLE: Begin!

RICKY: Could gum up the works.

SHAUNELLE: Start!

RICKY: Could throw me outta whack.

SHAUNELLE: YOU ARE OUTTA WHACK!!! COMMENCE!!!

RICKY: Pipe down, will ya?

(He whips the gun towards her head and pulls the trigger [click]. It seems to be routine for both parties. No commotion.)

RICKY: If you panic like this when the time comes, our asses are gonna be grass. *(Playing the Hollywood desperado)* Hey Sheriff, turn an' meet yer maker.

SHAUNELLE: *(Exasperated)* No...no...no...

RICKY: No?

SHAUNELLE: Beazley'd go for his heater if he heard that.

RICKY: Could be.

SHAUNELLE: You gotta speak to him with respect. Catch him unawares, as the sayin' goes. It's gotta be simple.

RICKY: I can handle that.

SHAUNELLE: No comment.
It's gotta sound like you're askin' directions or somethin'. Then when he turns, I deliver the line, not you. This here's *my* show!

RICKY: Right, you're the victim, you pull the trigger.

SHAUNELLE: Not a "victim". I'm a survivor. Now, after I deliver the line, I plug 'im!

RICKY: O K, here goes. *(Pause)* Say, sheriff...

SHAUNELLE: He turns. *(To the imaginary target, then she pulls the trigger)* Meetcher maker, macho man! Bang!!! *(Click)*

(She smiles and blows imaginary smoke from the barrel then hands the gun to him.)

SHAUNELLE: C'mon, this here's our last kiss on earth.

(They kiss passionately. Then he raises the gun to her head.)

RICKY: Bang!!! *(Click)*

*(*SHAUNELLE *falls "dead" on the couch.* RICKY *raises the pistol to his open mouth.* SHAUNELLE*—who has been watching with one eye open and head tilted upwards—leaps up as* RICKY *delivers an open-mouthed...)*

RICKY: —Ang!!! *(Click. As he's falling)* Oh Lord, I'm a goner!

SHAUNELLE: No, no, godammit!!! Not in the mouth. The temple. That's all we need. Some a these criminal psychologists will start puttin' all kinds'a dumb pieces together. With you bein' a half 'n half an' an ex-con. No tellin' what conclusions they'll tell the world.

RICKY: What're you talkin' about?

SHAUNELLE: A gun's a sexual symbol.

RICKY: *(Dumbfoundedly examining the gun from various angles)* It don't do nothin' for me.

SHAUNELLE: Look, what we're aimin' for is a simple murder an' love suicide. That's all. Nothin' complicated.

RICKY: I was just tryna put some life inta it.

SHAUNELLE: Life is what we *don't* want.

RICKY: I wanted to jazz it up some, like Albert Hitchcock might.

SHAUNELLE: Try it again and cut the post-mortem speechifyin'. If ya shoot yerself in the dome, yer hardly gonna say, "Lord, I'm a goner."

RICKY: Well, I'm not gonna say, "Hot diggidy!"

SHAUNELLE: I don't want *any* speech.

RICKY: "Lord, I'm a goner", is hardly a speech. It's not like I'm recitin' the Gettysburg Add—

SHAUNELLE: Again!!!

RICKY: *(Resuming their positions, he hands her the gun.)* Say, Beazley—

SHAUNELLE: *Sheriff* Beazley! Let him think ya respect him.

RICKY: Say, Sheriff Beazley...

SHAUNELLE: He turns. *(Beat)* Meetcher match, macho man. Bang!!! *(Click)*

(She smiles. They kiss.)

RICKY: This is fun.

SHAUNELLE: We're not here t'have fun. This here's serious business. Continue with the ritual.

RICKY: *(Raising the gun to his own temple)* Bang!!! *(Click. He collapses.)*

SHAUNELLE: *(In utter despair)* Oh, God... why me??? Why me???

RICKY: Ya said the temple. *(Pointing to the side of his head)* What's 'is, my bellybutton?

SHAUNELLE: *Me* first! *(Beat)* Have you got a mental block?

RICKY: About bumpin' myself off? Well...yeah, as a matter of fact.

SHAUNELLE: Well, I can't cater t'your selfish whims. We're gonna get this straight if it kills us.

RICKY: If that's a joke, it went over like a fart in church. Anyway, I was tryin' somethin' out. Like an experiment.

SHAUNELLE: Get the fundamentals down. Then ya can experiment.

RICKY: Well, what if *I* went first?

SHAUNELLE: Beazely goes first.

RICKY: Me first, on our side.

SHAUNELLE: I can't even think about that.

RICKY: I'm confused. You got the death wish but I gotta pull the trigger.

SHAUNELLE: Death is not a wish. It's a fact. We're all gonna die.

RICKY: But not by our own hands.

SHAUNELLE: *(Increasingly distraught)* I'm not. I'm dyin' by yours. An' I told you, you don't hafta croak yourself. That doesn't hafta be a part of it.

RICKY: But I can't live without you. You're all I've ever had.

SHAUNELLE: All you've ever had? You've had plenty of girls.

RICKY: You're all I ever loved. You go, I go.

SHAUNELLE: Remember, I never planned death for you.

RICKY: Or me for you. We're victims of blind desire.

SHAUNELLE: Well, I like the sound of that. However, if you went first, I might wind up in a looney bin.

RICKY: I'd be on ice an' you'd be on lithium.

SHAUNELLE: Nobody'd win.

RICKY: Who's winnin' the way we're playin' it now?

SHAUNELLE: Try again without the experiments. We can't leave a thing to your imagination. It's gotta be instinct. Like a dog takin' a pee.

RICKY: Don't compare our lives to a dog takin' a pee. An' I'll have the routine by the time we get there.

SHAUNELLE: Then it's too late. See how close we are. *(Pointing to the "X" on the map)*

RICKY: Less than an inch.

SHAUNELLE: *(Fingering two adjacent spots on the map)* We are here an' our destination is—

RICKY: Our ron-day-voo with destiny. That sounds better.

SHAUNELLE: Right! I like that. Our rendezvous is right down the road, almost. So, one more time, now. Maybe we can practice some more when Lu Rae's out on the bally.

RICKY: Rehearsal. We decided it was a—

SHAUNELLE: I know. I know. Come on.

(They go through the ritual one more time. RICKY gets it straight. They lay prone for a moment. Then SHAUNELLE pops up.)

SHAUNELLE: We're missin' something.

RICKY: Not by my accountin'.

SHAUNELLE: How will they know it's a love suicide and not a murder suicide.

RICKY: Nah, people who know us...they know we're too much in love for murder. I mean, we punch each other around ever-so-often but—

SHAUNELLE: The coroner don't know us. He'll call it a crime of passion.

RICKY: Well, ain't it?

SHAUNELLE: It's a crime of love. Love an' passion are different. Passion is X-rated. Love is P G.

RICKY: Well, we could leave a note. We could pin it to Beazley's chest. Better yet, we could stab it to his chest.

SHAUNELLE: Notes're impersonal. An' they answer unanswered questions. That destroys the mystery. Anyway, only a poet could do justice to a note like that.

RICKY: You're a kinda poet.

SHAUNELLE: I only got the instincts, not the words. But a picture is worth a thousand words.

RICKY: I dunno. I seen pitchers I wouldn't give ya two words for, much less two cents.

SHAUNELLE: We gotta be arm-in-arm when the cops find us. So tight they gotta bury us in the same coffin. Like this. *(She hugs him...)* Tighter!

(He reciprocates. They grunt...)

SHAUNELLE: That's more like it.

RICKY: Maybe if I get on top an' you scissor your legs around me like when we make love—

SHAUNELLE: Good idea.

RICKY: Maybe we oughtta be makin' love for real.

SHAUNELLE: No...no...break!

(As they're separating)

SHAUNELLE: Then it becomes pornography. We want *erotic,* not neurotic... love, not lust... devotion, not deviation. Anyway, I don't know if we'd be aroused with Beazley lyin' there oozin' blood. You have trouble enough gettin' it up under normal cir—

RICKY: *(Snapping angrily)* Only when I'm drunk!!!

SHAUNELLE: Anyway, we'd be losin' too much time takin' off our duds.

RICKY: That's a point. *(Beat)* Look, don't Pentecostal Baptist have rules against suicides?

SHAUNELLE: Carny's my religion, now.

RICKY: We gotta shoot Beazley but why do we hafta shoot ourselves?

SHAUNELLE: I repeat, we'd never get outta town alive.

RICKY: I ain't disputin' our fate. The handwritin's onna floor. Our geese are cooked. I just question our method, that's all.

SHAUNELLE: It's quick. Clean.

RICKY: Clean? Blood all over each other's heads...faces. That's clean? Momma said if I chose to lead a life a'crime, please come home in an open casket. We oughtta try poison.

SHAUNELLE: *Try* poison? This ain't menu A and menu B.. Poison takes too long. An' it's too tame. I wanna go out inna blaze of glory. *(Pensively)* I never had a blaze of glory.

RICKY: A blaze of glory's overrated. With poison we could simply drift off.

SHAUNELLE: I don't wanna drift off simply. My whole life's been about simply driftin'. I wanna be remembered for somethin' dramatic...somethin' that rivets people t'the T V or paper. Jesus didn't make his big splash preachin'. He did it hangin' from mahogony.

RICKY: What's next fer you? Resurrection?

SHAUNELLE: If there's reincarnation, I won't come back as a kootchie. I'm comin' back as an owner. An' your notion of death by poison is right outta *Sayonara*.

RICKY: I dunno that I ever been there.

SHAUNELLE: It's a movie, dumbo.

RICKY: Well, I ain't heavy inta suicide research, like you. Or movies.

SHAUNELLE: 'Member when you were in jail last year an' I wrote an' tole ya about Baby Doll? How she killed herself?

RICKY: How could I forget?

SHAUNELLE: Well, she died by poison. If you believe that was painless, you believe in the tooth fairy. Baby Doll's intestines were all over her trailer. An' with her weighin' in at seven hundred and eighteen pounds, that was a helluva batch of intestines.

RICKY: You didn't write me *that*, Shaun. The boys woulda perked up over that story.

SHAUNELLE: I wasn't up to givin' the details. Baby Doll was my pal.

RICKY: Baby Doll was the only freak I ever heard of, committed suicide.

SHAUNELLE: Me, too. But Baby knew she was dyin' from the weight. It was self-inflicted euthanasia.

RICKY: Well, I guess we're gonna be kinda unique. A double carny suicide. A carnycide. *(He smiles at his little joke, then the smile fades)* Why am I smilin'?

SHAUNELLE: Nobody ever gets away who's a cop killer. Every flatfoot in America'll have his eye peeled for us. It's more romantic this way. Ya seen what happened t'Bonnie an' Clyde . Swiss cheese.

RICKY: Don't talk food after the Baby Doll story.

SHAUNELLE: Some of the great love stories in history ended like this. Hero and Leeander, Tristan and Eyesold, Romeo and Juliet...among others.

RICKY: Them last two, they made us read about them in high school.

SHAUNELLE: Like it?

RICKY: No way. Alla that stabbin' an' such. No wonder I gotta criminal streak.

SHAUNELLE: Izzat why ya never finished high school?

RICKY: High school was interruptin' my education. So ya been goin' to alla them local libraries studyin' up on love suicides.

SHAUNELLE: I may not be well-rounded but I am well read. Y'know, sometimes I wish you were Japanese. It's a noble tradition with Japanese.

RICKY: I think I'm bein' more than helpful. I'm not about to turn Jap.

SHAUNELLE: Anyway, carnies kill themselves with drinkin', drugs, AIDS... It's only the freaks seem content.

RICKY: That sure seems odd.

SHAUNELLE: Freaks *are* odd. That's why they're freaks. Like The Baron. Born three-feet-four inches.

RICKY: *Born* three-feet-four inches?

SHAUNELLE: Born to *grow* three-feet-four inches. But he never pitied himself. He lifted weights...judo-fought anyone who insulted him. Never backed down from anyone. He got ice water in his veins.

(LU RAE *enters eating an ice cream cone and heads for the trailer.*)

RICKY: Maybe The Baron would like to do Beazley in.

SHAUNELLE: You lily-livered louse! Why in God's name -

(*Defensively,* RICKY *points the pistol at her.* LU RAE *enters, misinterprets what she sees and screams one word in "carny".*)

LU RAE: MEE-A-ZUR, DEE-A-ZUR!
MEE-A-ZUR, DEE-A-ZUR!
MEE-A-ZUR, DEE-A-ZUR!

(RICKY *swings the gun at* LU RAE, *half in panic, half in irritation. He "fires" [Click]. She collapses—face first—in her ice cream.*)

SHAUNELLE: *(To* RICKY*)* Now you did it, you idiot!

(She rushes to her stepdaughter)

RICKY: *(Almost elated)* Amazin'... Amazin'! That was carny talk?

SHAUNELLE: Get some cold water, stupid.

RICKY: She's got her kisser buried in ice cream. What's colder than that? I mean who's the stupid one, here?

SHAUNELLE: Get it!!!

(He hustles to the sink and pours a glass of water.)

SHAUNELLE: *(To* LU RAE, *nestling her head)* It's O K, baby. You'll be arright. He didn't mean no harm.

*(*LU RAE *groans as* RICKY *crosses. He raises the glass above* LU RAE's *head and lets the water trickle onto her face.)*

RICKY: Amazin! Amazin!

SHAUNELLE: Gimmee that, you stupid shit!!!

(Grabbing the glass and tossing the water in LU RAE's *face.)*

LU RAE: *(Leaping up)* Holy guacamole! *(Examining her body)* Did he get me???

SHAUNELLE: No, no, baby! It's O K.

LU RAE: Did he get *you*?

RICKY: Amazin'! ...Amazin'!

SHAUNELLE: Shut yer stupid face!

RICKY: Why's she bein' so mellerdramatic? Did she think I was gonna drill 'er?

LU RAE: Cause my daddy used to do that. 'Member, Shaunelle?

SHAUNELLE: I remember, baby.

LU RAE: He'd be loaded an' the gun would be loaded.

RICKY: Mine ain't loaded.

LU RAE: HOW DO I KNOW THAT???

RICKY: Cause I asked you to buy some bullets.

LU RAE: Oh, yeah. They're in my bag. You owe me eighteen dollars and forty-three cents. Plus the ice cream cone.

RICKY: Eighteen dollars an'...! These bullets ain't for The Lone Ranger!

LU RAE: NO SHIT!!! *(To* SHAUNELLE*)* 'Member how he used t'do that t'us?

SHAUNELLE: I remember, honey. Only I didn't cry.

LU RAE: Yeah, wouldn't give him the satisfaction. *(Beat)* What'd you ever see in my father?

SHAUNELLE: I dunno. You do some crazy things when yer lonely

LU RAE: I always thought if he was gonna plug one of us, it'd be me. I was the cry baby. But you were tough...just like him.

SHAUNELLE: Bein' a bully to a scared little girl ain't tough.

RICKY: I'm sorry I scared ya, Lu Rae.

LU RAE: It's O K, Ricky. You just don't know any better.

(LU RAE exits to the bedroom and her mother is left to wipe up the ice cream. Next door, the girl will whip clothing out of the closet, scattering it about. She finds what she wants and enters the bathroom. Meanwhile BARNEY rushes on carrying a knife and bursts into the trailer.)

BARNEY: What's goin' on here? Who yelled "Murder"?

SHAUNELLE: It's O K, Barney. Everythin's under control.

BARNEY: That's what ya get fer beddin' down with a jailbird.

SHAUNELLE: It's not "beddin' down" when yer married t'him.

RICKY: *You* married us!

BARNEY: Don't remind me.

RICKY: Anyway, I paid my debt in the eyes of the law.

BARNEY: T'hell you did. What about my weddin' bill?

RICKY: I'm payin' that.

BARNEY: Only after I started takin' it outta your salary.

SHAUNELLE: At one hundred percent interest.

RICKY: You want me broke. A real preacher wouldn'a charged two hundred bucks t'get married.

BARNEY: I'm more'n a real preacher. I take care of ya.

SHAUNELLE: You *control* us.

BARNEY: Not you, Shaunelle. If I controlled you, things'd be a lot different around here. *(To RICKY)* An' a real preacher couldn'a married you onna carousel. Precious little thanks ya showed. Pukin' yer lunch up at the exchange of the rings.

RICKY: I get motion sickness.

(LU RAE re-enters. Her face is clean and her blouse is unbuttoned down the back. She is braless.)

BARNEY: *(Heading out)* Cut the horseplay. Get ready for dinner. Shaunelle, step out here fer a second, will ya?

(SHAUNELLE crosses and leaves the trailer with BARNEY. He leads her as far away as possible. Meanwhile, LU RAE and RICKY converse.)

LU RAE: He still got the hots fer Ma.

RICKY: Let him get his own woman.

LU RAE: Don't knock it. His itch fer her is how you landed this gig. Button me up, will ya. *(Turning her back to him)*

RICKY: Why you always askin' me to do this?

LU RAE: You button up Shaunelle, don'tcha?

RICKY: Thass different.

LU RAE: Variety's the spice of life.

RICKY: It's not proper.

LU RAE: What's proper??? Start buttonin'.

(He does so, reluctantly. She leans into him. Meanwhile, outside...)

BARNEY: Everythin' arright in your life, Shaunnelle?

SHAUNELLE: Peaches 'n cream. A bowl a'cherries. Did Ricky say somethin's afoot?

BARNEY: When Ricky talks, I go deaf. *(He hands her a telegram.)* A telegram from that big clinic in Minnesota.

SHAUNELLE: *(Grabbing it)* Not a word! Keep this onna Q T! It's ...uh, my pet charity. My daddy died there.

BARNEY: I thought you said you never knew yer daddy.

SHAUNELLE: *(Nervously)* Aw, no...I was speakin'...y'know, figurative.

BARNEY: I'd foot yer bills iffn you were sick. I feel closer t'you than any of the rest.

SHAUNELLE: I ain't sick. I ain't even hit my prime, yet.

BARNEY: Ain't that a cancer clinic?

(SHAUNELLE races into the trailer, past LU RAE and RICKY into the bedroom. BARNEY registers a look of profound heartbreak, then exits.)

RICKY: *(Calling after SHAUNELLE)* He didn't touch you, did he?

SHAUNELLE: *(She slams the door as she utters...)* Nah...nah...nah...

(She reads the telegram as the others talk in the next room. When she's finished, she registers great pain. She rips up the telegram, takes a deep breath and tries to compose herself.)

LU RAE: *(To* RICKY*)* Hey, what the hell was so amazin' t'you?

RICKY: It's amazin' how you reacted to the gun. You screamed out "Murder, Murder, Murder" in carny. Now, that's shrewd.

LU RAE: It's my native language, fer Chrissakes. When ya panic, ya go back to childhood. Like soldiers in a war movie. When the gooks are closin' in, they say, "Momma...Momma..."

RICKY: In real life they say, "Lemmee the fuck outta here!"

LU RAE: *(Popping a pill or two as* SHAUNELLE *re-enters)* If I yelled plain ole "Murder", then I wouldn'ta got any attention. Carnies would just figure that some mark bitch was in trouble. Prob'ly gettin' what's comin' to her.

RICKY: Yeah, ya gotta point.

SHAUNELLE: Hey, speakin' of which, what'd you find out?

LU RAE: Beazley's still sheriff. Big as life. But he looks pretty harmless t' me. Just a teddy bear.

SHAUNELLE: A grizzly bear.

LU RAE: Stops for a few beers onna way home at Junior's Dew Drop Inn. A roadhouse off alone by itself. I cased the joint. I figure ya rip out the phone inna parkin' lot an' in his cop car. Beazley can't call for help after you beat the shit outta him.

RICKY: Beat the shit outta him?

LU RAE: *(Excitedly)* Ya conjurin' up somethin' better?

SHAUNELLE: *(Interjecting)* Naw, naw, Ricky's just gonna whup Beazley's ass.

LU RAE: Let the air outta his tires an you guys'll be headed for Canada while I'm steerin' the cops t' Mexico. Hot damn!

SHAUNELLE: You act like this is gonna be some sorta picnic or somethin'.

LU RAE: Well, it's gonna be fun, ain't it?

RICKY: Fun? I don't see any fun comin' around the horizon.

SHAUNELLE: *(Intensely)* Satisfaction!

LU RAE: Excitement, then! Adventure. I just wish I could string along for the getaway.

SHAUNELLE: Outta the question. You stay with the show. We'll hook up later. This ain't some sorta game we're playin'.

LU RAE: Sort of a game.

SHAUNELLE: I used t'think like you but I wised up.

LU RAE: Y'mean, you crossed the line, Shaunelle. That wised you up. Risky way for a kootch t'learn a lesson. See, I never cross the line.

RICKY: What line?

LU RAE: If that wasn't enough, ya did the "greasy pole".

RICKY: What "greasy pole"?

LU RAE: Look, what happened t'you last year was a terrible thing.

SHAUNELLE: Enough.

LU RAE: But ya gotta admit, you'd heat the customers up.

RICKY: What line?

LU RAE: You'd cross the line an' you'd let 'em touch ya. There's always one creep who thinks you're ready fer anythin'. An' that night it happened t' be Beazley.

SHAUNELLE: Shut up, Lu Rae.

LU RAE: Didn't ya learn when that guy up in Canada bit ya onna thigh?

RICKY: What "greasy pole"???

LU RAE: So when Beazley saw you were doin' the greasy pole...well, the cop figgered you were fair game.

RICKY: What "line"?

SHAUNELLE: He's gonna pay in spades.

RICKY: What "greasy pole"???

LU RAE: Beazley probably figgered it was bein' offered. Maybe he was readin' you right.

SHAUNELLE: Put a cork in yer trap!

LU RAE: It's a free country...so they tell me.

SHAUNELLE: Shut up!

RICKY: WHAT "GREASY POLE"???

LU RAE: I got rights as a citizen!

SHAUNELLE: SHUT UP, LU RAE!!!

RICKY: WHAT "GREASY POLE"???

SHAUNELLE: SHEE-A-ZUT, EE-A_ZUPP!
SHEE-A-ZUT, EE-A-ZUPP!
SHEE-A-ZUT, EE-A-ZUPP!

(Everything subsides. LU RAE is frightened, SHAUNELLE is livid and RICKY is confused. After a pause...)

RICKY: *(Quietly to LU RAE)* Does that mean, "Shut up"?

(LU RAE nods. RICKY continues...)

RICKY: I figgered as much.

LU RAE: Those biphetamines don't do it fer you, Shaunelle. They're supposed to lift you up.

SHAUNELLE: I'd like to lift you up and throw you!!!

LU RAE: I dunno why I'm with you. I shoulda been raised by blood kin.

SHAUNELLE: Like your *daddy*?

LU RAE: Well... yeah. He's a tender, caring, sensitive fatherly type.

SHAUNELLE: And where is he?

LU RAE: Who knows?

(SHAUNELLE exits to the bedroom, flops on the bed and weeps.)

RICKY: Lu Rae, you're bein' mean-spirited to your momma.

LU RAE: She's not my momma. She just married my daddy. *(Beat...shrugs)* "The line" is a strip a'tape across the stage three feet from the edge. Our boundary line. The "greasy pole" is...well, uh...a kinda raunchy routine that respectable, ladylike kootchies—like me—don't do.

RICKY: I thought all you did was strip an' dance around some.

LU RAE: Not Shaunelle. She gave the boys their money's worth in her day.

RICKY: Geez, if I'da known that I'da put a stop t'it.

LU RAE: From where? From jail? You wouldn'a known even if you were hereabouts. That's why carnies ain't allowed to watch kootchie.

RICKY: That's a dumb-ass rule.

LU RAE: It's the best rule onna midway. What would happen if you heard the marks reactin' to the girls. The blood would flow like water. We depend on you guys fer protection. How you gonna respect us if you see us flashin' in fronta three hundred strangers?

RICKY: We know you do it.

LU RAE: Knowin' ain't seein'!

RICKY: I'm gonna have me a word with The Queen of Sheba!

SHAUNELLE: *(Emerging)* Forget it! I don't do kootchie anymore, remember?

RICKY: I thought you was providin' innocent pleasure out there onna bally. Naughty...but innocent.

SHAUNELLE: Look, I paid for this trailer from the dollars those marks would offer. Don't forget that.

LU RAE: Tell Ricky how ya collected those doll—

SHAUNELLE: An' don't you forget it either, little bigmouth!

LU RAE: I'll soon have my own trailer. Then you won't hafta listen t'little bigmouth, anymore.

SHAUNELLE: Can't happen soon enough for me. If it happens at all. Ya gotta great body, hon. But ya don't know how t'kootch. Ya can't even do the bump an' grind.

LU RAE: *(Subdued)* I can bump. An I can...grind.

SHAUNELLE: Bullshit! Ya look like yer sufferin' from stomach cramps up there. You grind like yer in traction. An' that expression on yer face... can't you at least, *look* like you're enjoyin' yourself?

LU RAE: I *am* enjoyin' myself!

SHAUNELLE: Yer stoned outta yer skull.

LU RAE: We're all stoned!

(A bell clangs [off]).

LU RAE: Dinner. Let's head for the Z-top.

RICKY: Hot damn! I love t'eat!

SHAUNELLE: How long did your trip take?

LU RAE: Coupla hours. We only gotta stop at Maple Grove State Fair before we're there.

SHAUNELLE: I know! Believe me! I've memorized the route.

RICKY: That shames me. If you can learn the route, why can't I get down the ritual?

LU RAE: What ritual?

RICKY: Why, the ritual that—

SHAUNELLE: *(Glaring at him)* Get yer butt inta gear, Ricky! *(To* LU RAE*)* You comin'?

LU RAE: Yeah, lemmee wash up, will ya?

(SHAUNELLE exits, RICKY in tow. LU RAE stares after them then to herself...)

LU RAE: What ritual? *(Beat)* I'm bein left outta somethin', I suspect.
(She shrugs after a pause. She then bumps...one...two...three times) I can bump
t' perfection. *(She tries vainly to grind. She repeats and again fails. Trying
again...)* I wonder if I gotta slipped disc. *(Beat)* I wonder where yer disc is.
(Beat) I wonder what makes a disc slip. *(Beat)* I wonder where yer disc goes
when it slips.

*(She clutches the small of her back in pain as the lights fade and the music comes
up.)*

END OF ACT ONE

ACT TWO

(The same. That night)

(We hear the sounds of an offstage commotion [police sirens, general mayhem]. This will keep up—under the onstage voices—for a few minutes. After a moment, RICKY then SHAUNELLE rush on, out of breath. Theyre in a state of disarray i.e. his wig and beard are disheveled and out of place. He carries his breast and woman's shoe. His make-up is smeared. The bottom of SHAUNELLE's costume is nowhere in sight. She's barefoot and in tights under her robe.)

SHAUNELLE: Ricky, wait up! Where's the fire?

RICKY: *(Motioning off)* Back there!

SHAUNELLE: Boy, you sure hightailed it outta the ten-in-one after a smashing entrance.

RICKY: "When the tough get goin', the goin' get tough."

SHAUNELLE: Illustrated Ike says they sent out a six-county alarm.

RICKY: I never believe Ike. He's the one once said we was invited to The White House.

SHAUNELLE: Six counties. That'd include Beazley's turf. He may've already arrived t'quiet the riot.

RICKY: Maybe he'll get killed inna line of duty. That'd be real nice.

SHAUNELLE: Don't be morbid.

RICKY: Don't be morbid? *You're* settin' up a bloodbath.

SHAUNELLE: Duck inta the trailer. Between the marks and Beazley, I'm notorious...again.

RICKY: I wasn't cut out fer this game.

(They enter the trailer and close the door behind. SHAUNELLE locks.)

SHAUNELLE: Don't turn on the light. If Lu Rae comes home, we'll open. Meanwhile, we got our own asses to preserve.

RICKY: Far as I'm concerned, she can sleep under a tree, tonight *(Beat)* Whataya mean, "*If* she comes home"? We're all she's got.

SHAUNELLE: She's havin' a ball. You know how she feels about danger...excitement. She gets revved up when action's comin' down.

RICKY: Maybe it's just as well she's not here bitchin' an' bellyachin' about her momma.

SHAUNELLE: I did what I'm paid to do.

RICKY: All she gotta hear is that the riot started in the ten-in-one. She'll figure it started over you.

(SHAUNELLE starts dressing. RICKY will start taking off his make-up.)

SHAUNELLE: It started over my costume. My seam split open alla way down my leg. I'll protest my innocence t'my dyin' day.

(RICKY sighs. SHAUNELLE reacts...)

SHAUNELLE: I mean...I'll protest my innocence t'beat the band. How's at?

RICKY: Even if mermaids were real, Barney wouldna sprung fer one.

SHAUNELLE: If I wasn't fake, none of those carnies'd be layin' in hospitals. Or worse, even.

RICKY: It was fate.

SHAUNELLE: Thass what I just said.

RICKY: Fate! F-A-T-E! Fate dealt carnies a cruel blow tonight. Damn, it's tough seein' under this light.

SHAUNELLE: What light?

RICKY: Well, under this lack a'light.

SHAUNELLE: I ain't been this scared in a year. It's like I was facin' a tent fulla Beazleys.

RICKY: 'Cept those boys tonight...they weren't in it fer sex.

SHAUNELLE: Sez who? Who knows what woulda happened if you hadn'ta rushed in...bashin' marks...left an' right...pillar t'post? You were a heller, honey.

RICKY: Offense is the best defense. *(Proudly)* Learned that in jail.

SHAUNELLE: A mark's no match fer Ricky Roo.

RICKY: *(Peering out the window)* Things're windin' down.

SHAUNELLE: At least we get off a little early tonight.

RICKY: You think Barney's gonna close down just cause of a riot?

SHAUNELLE: You seen what's it's like out there. Goddam jungle!

RICKY: Doesn't bother Barney if there's a buck t'be made. This all coulda been avoided iffn he gave those boys a refund.

SHAUNELLE: You can't give a sucker back his dough. Be hell t'pay. The freaks have made an honest livin' from their deformities. An' the self-mades have spent years on their gimmick. If they don't get paid cause the riot started over a rigged act...cause of a fake...well, my life might not be worth a plugged nickel.

RICKY: Nah! We're all carnies. It's us against the straight world. Besides, your life...our lives ain't gonna be worth a plugged nickel, anyways.

SHAUNELLE: But at least we're in control of our own destinies.

RICKY: If we was in control of our own destinies, we wouldn't be talkin' suicide.

SHAUNELLE: *Love* suicide! There's a considerable difference between suicide and love suicide.

RICKY: None that I can see.

SHAUNELLE: One's on accounta despair, the other's on accounta desire. They're poles apart.

RICKY: Dead is dead. Period!

SHAUNELLE: All you ever think on is yerself.

RICKY: Jee-zuss! I don't believe what I'm hearin'!

SHAUNELLE: Self-pity's a bore. Why not pity Prince Electro? He may not pull through. Critical condition. All because of me.

RICKY: Because of yer *costume*. Anyway, The Prince shoulda stuck t'sword swallowin'. That ain't dangerous enough?

SHAUNELLE: Neon tubes're more graphic. When he swallows the tube then turns on the switch an' ya see the glow in his stomach...well, that's a sight.

RICKY: That's a helluva illusion.

SHAUNELLE: It ain't an illusion. It's a fact.

RICKY: An' it's all ruined by a punch from a punk t'his belly.

SHAUNELLE: An' Fuego The Fire Eater. Pity him a bit while yer at it. He was doin' "The Fountain of Flame" an' he hadda mouthful a'kerosene. Only the riot breaks his concentration an' all of a sudden, his face goes up in flames. He'll be arright. But I betcha he never does the Fountain of Flame again.

RICKY: Zenobia chopped up her boa constrictor when he panicked an' broke her ribs. She kept moanin', "What have I done t'Bobo, my boa?"

SHAUNELLE: I have very little pity for a woman who loves a snake.

RICKY: It was a true crime of passion.

SHAUNELLE: The Baron's gotta concussion.

RICKY: *(Cynically)* What's in his coconut t'damage.

SHAUNELLE: *(Physically animating the description)* The mark bastards were tryna pull the beard offa Lucy. No dice, of course. So, they strip her to prove she's a guy. No dice, again. So, she's cryin' an' screamin' an' tryna cover up when The Baron storms in with his gang of shrimps. They're swingin' chains an' bats an' clubs.

RICKY: Fair's fair. None of 'em's even four feet tall. They's levelin' the playin' field.

SHAUNELLE: But one of 'em grabs The Baron by the ankles an' uses him fer battin' practice. Cherry Vanilla ran an' got Nikolai The Knife Thrower. He nailed the mark inna stomach from a hundred feet or so.

RICKY: I'd *never* mess with Nikolai. *(Beat)* You wanna drink?

SHAUNELLE: Yeah, I could use one.

(He crosses and opens the refrigerator. She rushes across shouting...)

SHAUNELLE: THE LIGHT!!!

(She slams the door on his fingers. He howls. She desperately tries to quiet him, her hand on his mouth.)

RICKY: *(Blowing on his fingers and speaking through the pain)* Nothin's gonna happen causa some dinky little light.

SHAUNELLE: Oh, yeah? If Mr. Paul Revere believed that, we'd be sippin' tea an' crimpets.

RICKY: *(Still smarting)* What's a crimpet?

SHAUNELLE: Biscuits,..like. I think.

RICKY: How inna hell can you sip biscuits?

(She unplugs the refrigerator, opens the door and gets two beers. She closes the door, reinserts the plug, pops the two beers and grabs a bag of potato chips.)

RICKY: Cops was beatin' on two ride boys cause they'd only speak "carny". All they'd say was, "Fee-a-zuk, yee-a-zou!" Cops can even figure out what that means.

SHAUNELLE: Ride boys are dumb.

RICKY: *(Sipping satisfactorily)* Our pre-dinner happy hour is my favorite time of day.

SHAUNELLE: Me, too. *Hors d'oeuvres? (Offering the chips)*

RICKY: They arrested The Bozo from "The Dump The Nigger" stand.

SHAUNELLE: *(Visibly irritated)* Nobody calls it *that*, anymore.

RICKY: Well, they may not call it that anymore. But that's what they mean. What are you gonna call it, "Dump The African-American" stand?

SHAUNELLE: They call it "Dump The Bozo".

RICKY: It just doesn't sound right. A tradition's a tradition. Even if The Bozo is a wetback.

SHAUNELLE: Ricky, if they put your brain inside a worm's head, it'd crawl backwards. Hey, what about The Bearded Lady?

RICKY: What about 'er?

SHAUNELLE: Did she make it to the z-top?

RICKY: I dunno.

SHAUNELLE: You dunno?

RICKY: I didn't see 'er.

SHAUNELLE: She wasn't there?

RICKY: She mighta been.

SHAUNELLE: I thought ya said ya didn't see 'er.

RICKY: Right.

SHAUNELLE: Then she wasn't there.

RICKY: That ain't necessarily so.

SHAUNELLE: If she was there, you'da seen 'er.

RICKY: Maybe.

SHAUNELLE: Maybe?

RICKY: I din't notice 'er.

SHAUNELLE: Oh. *(Beat)* Why din't ya say so?

RICKY: I thought I did.

SHAUNELLE: How could ya *not* notice a bearded lady? *(Beat)* How about The Three-Eyed Man?

RICKY: I din't see him, neither.

SHAUNELLE: Ya mean you din't *notice* him.

RICKY: Right...notice.

SHAUNELLE: I hope they found each other.

RICKY: Me, too. Nobody else'd have either one of 'em.

SHAUNELLE: If they're hurt, I'd be tempted to use this heater, prematurely.

RICKY: What makes them special t'you?

SHAUNELLE: You'd never understand.

RICKY: If you want vengeance, bushwack that motha who walloped Prince Electro.

SHAUNELLE: I'm not comfortable with avenging others.

RICKY: What??? After what you've been plannin'? Izzat you talkin'?

SHAUNELLE: It's a man's task, except in my own case. Then "vengeance is mine". To quote Jesus.

RICKY: Mickey Spillane, too.

SHAUNELLE: Triclops and The Bearded Lady are legendary... like saints. Maybe not to you. But to true carnies. (She animates this with the histrionics of a movie star wannabe) When I was just a li'l bitty tadpole, my folks were with Adamo Brothers Starlight International Show. Momma had a jam store, Poppa ran a hanky-pank. One day, Triclops an' Lucy arrived. They got stranded when American Variety went belly-up. Well, I figgered like you do now, that they were just a couple of God's shortchanged people. No big deal. Most people are, one way or another. Triclops caused a li'l bit of a stir causa the third eye in the middle of his forehead. Even the veterans—who thought they'd seen everythin' in the way of freaks— well, they were even taken aback. Bearded Ladies are pretty easy t'come by. But three-eyers... well, they ain't exactly found on every street corner. Anyway, everybody adjusted t'them an' they settled in. After awhile, I became attracted t'them. First thing I noticed was they never went anywheres without each other. Even when they went to the ten-in-one. He'd walk her to her booth an' then proceed t'his own. They'd do their exhibitions then they'd head back to their trailer, hand-in-hand. Just the way they do today. They didn't smoke or drink or curse. An' they had those same little flower boxes in alla the windows. They kept the trailer neat as a pin. Never fought...never raised their voices. That's rare in carny life, as we well know. An' it's unheard of in the straight world, from what I hear.

Anyways, after awhile they started t'ask me t'run errands. So I'd go inta the various towns for 'em cause they didn't wanna leave the grounds. You can imagine how the marks woulda reacted iffn the Three-Eyed Man and The Bearded Lady strolled through K-Mart. When I'd return with their stuff, I'd come to their front door and peer in. And quite often, I'd see 'em standin' stark still in each other's arms. Right inna middle of their cheery little livin' room. An' they had this look on their faces... a look that had nothin' to do with the deformity of their faces. The look had to do with... well...with ecstacy, I guess. Yeah, ecstacy was what it was. I didn't really know at the time what that feelin' was with two people. 'Cept from the movies. All I knew was the opposite. I could only draw on my own experience. An' whatever the opposite of ecstacy was, my parents had it in spades. I'd knock onna door an' they'd bring me in. They'd show me their pictures of their daughter. She was beautiful...truly lovely. No third eye. No beard. Just this gorgeous face. They tole me she had run away at an early age causa the embarrassment. That made me feel sad. But they weren't bitter...not even hurt, it seemed. They said it was best for the girl. Can ya imagine that? They said it was God's will, that they were happy just to have had 'er. I thought it was funny when they spoke of God. I knew they didn't go to church. I guess they had deeper feelin's. I do remember that every day...real early in the mornin'... before the townies woke up, they'd strool off alone together, hand-in-hand, like always. Towards some secluded spot. An' one time, I set out t'follow 'em. The sun hadn't even come up yet. But they had no trouble seein'. Then they'd raise their hands an' offer up these prayers to God. The sun musta been God to them cause it was just risin'. They went for a good twenty minutes with these prayers I never heard at any Pentecostal Baptist church. An' every last prayer was of thanksgivin'. Can you imagine that? A prayer of thanksgivin' for God's bestowed graces!!!

Amazin'! Then as they finished up with a long, loud "Amen!", they turned and kissed the longest kiss I ever seen. Not a soul kiss, y' understand. It was clean an' neat an' warm. Then like nothin' at all had happened, they turned and headed back. An' I knew beyond a shadow of a doubt, my life would never be quite the same again. Never again the same.

RICKY: *(Long pause)* That's weird.

SHAUNELLE: *(Dismayed)* Maybe we should all be a little more weird.

RICKY: We're weird enough as it is, thank you. *(Beat)* Maybe their kid was a basket baby.

SHAUNELLE: Huh?

RICKY: Maybe she was left on their doorstep in a basket. Maybe they even kidnapped the kid. Those religious nuts're the worst kind. *(Listening intently)* Sounds like it's all over.

(Unseen by the pair, BEAZLEY enters outside the trailer. He's smiling.)

SHAUNELLE: Let's rehearse.

RICKY: Huh?

SHAUNELLE: The ritual.

RICKY: *(Shrugs)* O K.

(He gets the pistol and hands it to her. They perform the ritual successfully [in double-time].)

SHAUNELLE: Terrific. Yer gettin' the hang of it.

BEAZLEY: *(Singing from outside the trailer)* "Shaunelle, Shaunelle, my lovely little belle. My pretty kootchie baby, you're the swellest of the swell."

(RICKY and SHAUNELLE freeze. As BEAZLEY approaches the trailer, they scamper for cover. The lawman peers inside then pulls out a flashlight and checks the interior out [through the window].)

BEAZLEY: Shaunelle,...you in there, honey? It's your ole pal an' paramour, Merle Beazley. 'Member? Merle The Pearl?

RICKY: *(Whispers in astonishment)* Merle The Pearl???

BEAZLEY: *(To himself)* Well, I guess I'll hafta leave a little love note.

(He sits on the steps to write. SHAUNELLE is clearly nervous. RICKY is clearly confused.)

BEAZLEY: "Dear Shaunelle, I've thought constantly of our tender evenings, last year. The mutual bliss we shared—"

SHAUNELLE: *(Whispering to RICKY)* Let's do it. Now!

RICKY: *(Whispering)* No, no, I ain't ready. 'Sides, I'm a little curious about—

SHAUNELLE: You ain't ready? We just practiced it successfully.

RICKY: "Rehearsed"! Anyway, I gotta get psyched. This ain't an everyday thing.

(LU RAE runs on carrying SHAUNELLE's tailfin. She wears a bespangled bikini and a sheer robe. As she heads for the trailer, BEAZLEY intercepts her as he pulls his gun. She stops in fear. RICKY and SHAUNELLE listen, guardedly.)

BEAZLEY: Who's there? This here's the police.

LU RAE: *(Frightened)* It's only me. Little Lu Rae. Please don't shoot.

BEAZLEY: *(Jovially)* Oh, Lu Rae. Shaunelle's little girl. Why, it's Merle Beazley. Her friend from last year. 'Member? When she played my town down the road apiece?

LU RAE: What's the gun fer?

BEAZLEY: Oh sorry, force a'habit, I guess. *(But the gun stays drawn)* Where's yer momma, by the way?

LU RAE: Uh...uh...last I seen 'er, she was up at the z-top. Fixin' t'grub down. Just a minute ago.

BEAZLEY: I musta missed 'er.

LU RAE: *(Pointing at the gun)* P-p-please, guns scare me.

BEAZLEY: *(Without holstering the pistol)* Oh, that's interestin' t'know.

LU RAE: Shaunelle hid out when the riot started. Now that things are settlin', she come outta hidin'.

BEAZLEY: Well, I don't blame her none fer havin' hid. Those boys can get pretty randy an' rowdy. She'd be a likely target fer molestation. She sure is a pretty lady. You're gettin' t'be a pretty lil' gal yerself... in a different sorta...younger way than yer ma.

(He approaches and runs his fingers through her hair, the gun still drawn on nervous LU RAE. SHAUNELLE *and* RICKY *watch.)*

BEAZLEY: *(Lasciviously)* You'll be in my neck a'the woods, next week. Stop by an' see me. No need t'tell Shaunelle. I'll give you a ride in the car. I'll even let you wail the siren.

LU RAE: *(Cynically)* Am I gonna get handcuffed, too?

BEAZLEY: If ya savor that.

LU RAE: I'd savor time alone t'think about it.

BEAZLEY: Well, toodle-oo. I'm off. *(He exits)*

LU RAE: *(Quietly to herself)* She ain't really my ma. *(She runs to the trailer and knocks.)* Shaunelle! Ricky!

RICKY: *(Addressing her from the other side of the door)* Who's there?

LU RAE: Open the door, you dumb peckerwood bastard.

SHAUNELLE: *(To* RICKY*)* Open the door.

RICKY: You can't be too careful in times of crises.

(He opens. LU RAE *rushes for the bathroom tossing the tailfin at* SHAUNELLE.*)*

LU RAE: *(To* RICKY*)* Outta the way! I gotta go t'the donniker. *(She slams the bathroom door behind.)*

SHAUNELLE: *(Checking out the fin)* Wonder where she found this. *(Beat)* Guess we can turn on the light.

*(*RICKY *does so then looks at the clothing that* LU RAE*'s strewn about.)*

RICKY: Y'know, I think she needs a talkin' to.

SHAUNELLE: She won't listen t'me...t'nobody. Talk about what?

(He starts picking up the clothes and dumping them in the closet.)

RICKY: Neatness fer one thing. An' respect. I always had respect fer my elders.

SHAUNELLE: I ain't an elder!

RICKY: The names she calls me...the things she says to you...

SHAUNELLE: I raised her the best I could. I was out onna bally all night an' she was off on her own. Kootchyin' and motherin' aren't compatable. I'm lucky she's not in jail.

RICKY: Maybe she *should* spend time inna slammer. Gives ya a certain sense of responsibility. I'd think twice about leavin' everythin' t'Lu Rae. She ain't the appreciative type.

SHAUNELLE: Well, they say ya can't take it with ya.

RICKY: Y'know, that Beazley...well...he don't sound like no raper.

SHAUNELLE: You callin' me a liar?

RICKY: Nah. It's just that alla that sweet-talkin' he just been doin'—

SHAUNELLE: There were rapists in jail!!! Right???

RICKY: A' course.

SHAUNELLE: An' there were male rapists as well, huh?

RICKY: Certainly. What other kind are there?

SHAUNELLE: So, guys musta made advances at a good-lookin' stud like you?

RICKY: Yeah. But they was queers.

SHAUNELLE: How'd ya react t'that.

RICKY: How d'ya think? Like any normal fella. I broke a guy's jaw. Bit off a fella's ear.

SHAUNELLE: I thought you were a model con.

RICKY: I was.

SHAUNELLE: How'd they first approach you?

RICKY: From behind.

SHAUNELLE: No, what'd they first say t'you?

RICKY: Oh, they'd offer a cigarette or somesuch. I was always suspicious. I didn't smoke.

SHAUNELLE: An' you'd hear what a nice guy you were. Handsome t' boot.

(RICKY *nods. She continues...*)

SHAUNELLE: They were "sweet talkin'" you.

(RICKY *nods.*)

SHAUNELLE: Case closed. Beazley forced me to act out a courtin' relationship. He'd bring flowers...a little poem. Even forced me t'make dinner.

RICKY: That bastard. You *hate* makin' dinner.

SHAUNELLE: It was terrible. Then we'd have a couple a'drinks and then he'd make me... *(Indicating the bedroom in anguish)*

RICKY: Did you fight 'im?

SHAUNELLE: I couldn't. Throughout this whole...

RICKY: Ritual?

SHAUNELLE: No!!! We got the ritual!!! Throughout this whole...violation, he had his weapon out.

RICKY: Weapon?

SHAUNELLE: GUN!!! His .38 caliber revolver.

RICKY: Ya couldn't go t'the authorities. Who's gonna believe a kootchie? Especially one who got bit onna thigh for crossin' the line.

LU RAE: *(Emerging)* Wow! Whatta night! Hey Rick, pour me a drink, please.

RICKY: *(Extracting a beer from the refrigerator)* You're peaches an' cream when you want somethin'.

SHAUNELLE: Ya like what happened out there, tonight?

LU RAE: It was excitin'. It put some life inta this operation.

SHAUNELLE: Well, it mighta taken some life out before the night's over.

LU RAE: Y'mean, The Prince?

SHAUNELLE: 'Mong others.

LU RAE: He was livin' on borrowed time puttin' neon tubes down his throat.

SHAUNELLE: Geez, you don't even give a damn.

LU RAE: I give a damn, Ma. It's just that we all knew it would happen some day. I hope he pulls through. An' that he never does neon, again.

SHAUNELLE: If things were so excitin', why'd you come home?

LU RAE: Biological. They overturned alla the donnikers. Barney was sittin' in one. We nearly died laughin'.

RICKY: Could we cut down on the death talk?

LU RAE: You afraid a'death, Ricky?

RICKY: I don't exactly cotton t'it.

LU RAE: Death is not high in my scheme of things.

RICKY: Natcherly. Yer just a snot-nosed, little peanut.

LU RAE: I'm eighteen.

RICKY: Big deal!

SHAUNELLE: Have you seen Lucy?

LU RAE: Lucy?

SHAUNELLE: You don't even know their names. Just their handicaps. The Bearded Lady.

LU RAE: Oh, that's Lucy! Yeah, she was under the bally hidin' out like the rest of us. Her an' her three-eyed ole man.

SHAUNELLE: Triclops.

LU RAE: Arm-in-arm. Creepy sight.

SHAUNELLE: You're a real vessel of compassion.

LU RAE: Compassion's fer suckers. *(Beat)* She was wrapped in a blanket, bawlin' away. He was brushin' tears from her beard. Hell, those rioters wouldn'a been innerested in her. Only Triclops would get hot over a woman with a beard.

SHAUNELLE: SHE'S MORE THAN A BEARD!!! You'n Ricky can arm wrestle for the insensitivity award. *(Indicating the fin)* Where'd ya latch onta this?

LU RAE: One a'the roughies found it in a garbage can.

SHAUNELLE: It's not enough they molest ya. They trash yer costume as well.

LU RAE: You could at least, thank me for makin' this special trip.

SHAUNELLE: Thank you, thank you. You only come home t'take a leak.

LU RAE: An' t'tell ya we gotta finish the night.

SHAUNELLE: You gotta be kiddin'!!!

LU RAE: Barney spread a lotta green around. The cops're on our side, now. That's why we gotta do a late show. Harrelson figures we owe him.

SHAUNELLE: We owe him nothin! I gotta talk t' Barney Harrelson.

LU RAE: Hold yer water, Ma. Beazley's out there in search a' ya.

SHAUNELLE: I can take care a'him.

LU RAE: Like ya took care a'him last year?

(SHAUNELLE glares at her.)

RICKY: Yeah hon, I better go instead. Barney ain't itchin' t'talk t'ya.

SHAUNELLE: I can handle Barney, too. Hold the fort! *(She exits.)*

RICKY: If this was a fort, we wouldn'a hadda sit here inna dark.

LU RAE: If she pulls that roscoe on Beazley, it'll be suicide.

(RICKY flinches. She continues...)

SHAUNELLE: Still...if she got 'im alone...got the drop on him...
Ah, they'd catch up with 'er sooner or later. She'd savor the chase,
though. She's locked inta alla those movie fantasies. An' she wouldn't
care what happens to anyone else. She's such a selfish bitch.

RICKY: *(Beginning to see* LU RAE's *point)* Show some respect.

LU RAE: When she earns it. What'd she have t'do with that little to-do,
tonight?

RICKY: Nothin'.

LU RAE: Ricky!

RICKY: Not directly, at least.

LU RAE: Gimmee the "indirectly", then. It started in the ten-in-one.
The accusin' finger points t'her.

RICKY: Pretty women bring out the worst in mankind.

LU RAE: Yeah, she's real hot stuff. But I'm the one who suffers on accounta
her behavior.

RICKY: I only see you suffer when you practice yer bump 'n grind.

LU RAE: My grind! My grind! My bump's fine. She shoulda just up an' quit
carnie when she quit kootchyin'. But no, she gotta disrupt.

RICKY: It wasn't all her fault this time.

LU RAE: I thought she had nothin' to do with it.

RICKY: She was a victim, that's all.

LU RAE: We're all victims.

RICKY: Trouble follows 'er. I'm trouble an' I know it. I didn't wanna bring
hardship on Shaunelle, but... well, I just couldn't help myself. Be best iffn
I never came back when I got sprung. But, she's like a magnet t'me. Now
I'm in too deep t'turn back.

LU RAE: Turn back? From what?

RICKY: I'm trapped.

LU RAE: *(Becoming physical with him)* Trapped? What's trapped ya?

RICKY: You wouldn't understand.

LU RAE: *(Seductively)* Try me. *(Running her hands over her body)* I hear what
goes on every night as I lay out here on the foldaway. Ya call that bein
trapped? It drives me crazy. I toss an' squirm an' I do what a snappy
lookin' girl my age shouldn't hafta resort to. An' I'm fantasizin' 'bout you.

RICKY: I s'pose that's flatterin'.

LU RAE: You start my flights of fancy down the runway. I got passions... lusts...hungers...emotions...appetites...frenzies...

RICKY: O K, O K, you pretty well covered it.

LU RAE: I'd like to be trapped in a tender embrace every night.

RICKY: Tender embrace? My back feels like I been onna pirate ship. Anyway, what's t'keep you from gettin' a guy? Yer a good-lookin' girl.

LU RAE: What guy? Some hophead junkie ride boy? Some wino grifter. Some bindle stiff with V D. Gimmee a little dignity. Believe it or not, I'm practically a virgin.

RICKY: (Suppressing a laugh) G'wan.

LU RAE: Well, not countin the mistakes. An Im raisin my standards.

RICKY: Yer in the wrong business, then.

LU RAE: I'd have trouble leavin'. I hate marks.

RICKY: The right guy'll show up soon enough.

LU RAE: Soon enough is right now. Yer man enough fer both of us.

RICKY: Shaunelle's yer stepmother.

LU RAE: That ain't true kin.

RICKY: Anyways, I may steal but I don't cheat.

LU RAE: It's only a carny weddin'. An' I don't mind iffn yer hitched.

(Calliope starts up again.)

RICKY: D'you mind iffn Shaunelle minds?

LU RAE: Look, I admire yer faithfulness, Rick. It's pretty rare, nowadays. Especially fer a dude with a taste fer larceny. But what're you gonna do when Shaunelle's number is up?

RICKY: Wh... What number?

LU RAE: C'mon Rick, she's lucky she's alive after last year. If she tole the truth about Beazley. What's Ricky's game plan after she meets her maker?

RICKY: What's she been sayin' t'you?

(He grabs her.)

LU RAE: Nothin'. Nothin'. I just been observin'. If ever I seen a case of self-destruction-

RICKY: That ain't so! (Releasing her)

LU RAE: It ain't, huh? How come she just made out a will? What'sa woman her age doin' makin' out a will.

RICKY: *(Surprised)* She tell ya about the will?

LU RAE: She tole Barney t'tell me when the time come. But Barney can't keep his raggedy-ass, rat-shit trap shut. If she got you tied up in some dumb-ass scheme, you're gettin' the short end. Hell, ya made it through jail. An' with yer pretty face preserved.

RICKY: *(Without conviction)* Nah...Shaunelle...she don't have no scheme...afoot...that—

LU RAE: Suit yerself! Barney also thinks she's sick. Real sick!

RICKY: Physical? I dunno know nothin' about no sickness. How sick?

LU RAE: Mayo Clinic sick. She stopped off there when we played Minnesota. Then she startred talkin' about Beazley. *Six months* after the dastardly deed. How come it takes 'er six months t'say she got violated?

RICKY: I dunno. She does lotsa things late.

LU RAE: An' remember, she was a top carny stripper. Now she's fakin' a mermaid. See, I never believed that Beazley's *alleged* attack was reason to quit. The other day I seen 'er starin' at Cotton Candy Clara. Clara was a top kootch in 'er day.

RICKY: God, she's an ole hag.

LU RAE: Mom's agein'...sick. If she has a shootout with the cops—maybe puts Beazley t'sleep—she'll make T V and newspapers all over the country. Be a cinch fer a feature article in *Crime And Violence Monthly*. Maybe even a movie about her ill-fated life. That's her idea of fame.

RICKY: Most people never get movies made about themselves.

LU RAE: What good is it if they ain't around t'see it? Wake up, Ricky. The handwritin's on the tombstone.

(SHAUNELLE hurriedly re-enters and glances through the window as she prepares to enter the trailer.)

RICKY: Sure she didn't tell ya what she's been conjurin' up?

(Unaware that SHAUNELLE's observing, LU RAE grabs RICKY and kisses him passionately. RICKY resists...then gives in. Completely. SHAUNELLE looks away for a long, sad moment. But slowly she breaks into a wry, quiet smile...then a sort of satisfied discovery. She proceeds to bang on the door. The pair disentangles.)

RICKY: Who's there?

SHAUNELLE: Open up, Rick!

RICKY: *(Opening)* Pays to be careful.

SHAUNELLE: *(To LU RAE)* Well, you're right for once. He wants us out there. Barney don't care one whit or iota about his employees.

LU RAE: Whatcha complain' about? Ya brought this on yerself.

SHAUNELLE: Butt out, bigmouth! Go make up.

LU RAE: Bigmouth is right. I hadda talk the strippers outta comin' down here an' lowerin' the boom.

SHAUNELLE: (Grabbing the pistol) Yeah, well you just tell 'em they'll hafta lower the boom on *this* before they deal with me.

LU RAE: Ma, you get a little crazier every day.

SHAUNELLE: Look, yer profession calls. Go inta the donniker an' freshen' up.

LU RAE: This won't take long. A natural beauty don't need much makeup. (Exiting to the bathroom)

RICKY: She's startin' t'talk like you.

SHAUNELLE: Clam up, Ricky! He's on his way.

RICKY: Who is???

SHAUNELLE: Beazeley.

RICKY: B-B-Beazley??? Wh... Wh...what's he comin' here for?

SHAUNELLE: I talked him inta it. We can do it, tonight.

RICKY: *IT???*

SHAUNELLE: The ritual.

RICKY: The ritual? The real one? Tonight???

(She nods. He continues...)

RICKY: Aw no, Shaun. It ain't ready yet.

SHAUNELLE: It's a perfect situation. Lotsa newspaper people coverin' the riot. They'll write us up, too.

RICKY: I don't think I can psych myself in time. Why can't we—

SHAUNELLE: (Ignoring him) What a terrific set a'circumstances.

RICKY: H-H-How d'ya figger?

SHAUNELLE: One last rehearsal. Then we kick the kid outta here. When he sees her head toward the bally, he'll run down here. (Pointing out the window) I can't believe our luck.

RICKY: Luck???

SHAUNELLE: Life's a shitpit. Its time we got a break. We're God's shortchanged people.

RICKY: I'd rather get shortchanged than no change at all.

(She heads for the outside door. RICKY hesitates.)

RICKY: I better relieve myself. Better now than later.

SHAUNELLE: Yeah, that'd mess up the effect.

(She goes out the door and stands outside miming her fast draw. At a certain point, she'll check that she's unobserved, pull out a small box of bullets, extract two and put them in her pocket. She'll drop the empty box nearby and she'll throw the rest of the bullets off.)

(LU RAE emerges from the bathroom, ready for work. RICKY still holds the unloaded gun.)

LU RAE: Where's Ma?

RICKY: Gone out front.

LU RAE: Gone inna head, y'mean. Not like me. Izzt thing loaded? *Don't point it at me!*

(He does so, she panics and he sqeezes off a...click. She relaxes.)

RICKY: Empty.

LU RAE: So's yer noodle. I gotta warm up. *(She does stretching exercises)*

RICKY: Won't do ya no good, Lu Rae. You'll never learn t'grind.

LU RAE: The grind's been givin' me *beau coup* pain. But there's plenty of things I can do other than kootch. Even inna outside world. What's the point of bein' carny if yer not a "star"? An' I'd take care of ya since ya don't really have a profession. 'Cept fer stealin' an' ya flopped at that. I'm half her age... saner...prettier. I mean she ain't *old*, old. But hell, I'm just recently outta girlhood. So, drop yer brotherly ways. I'm a woman now, full-blooded. You'n me is all each other needs. Kiss me! *(She initiates a passionate kiss.)* Whataya say, Rick?

RICKY: *(Unhinged)* Well, I say that me'n yer ma have a bit a business. Afterwards, this joint'll be jumpin'.

LU RAE: Owwwww, sounds like fun.

RICKY: Don't bet the rent on it. Now, skeddadly up t' the bally.

LU RAE: You bet, baby.

(She rushes out and past SHAUNELLE.)

SHAUNELLE: Lu Rae, honey—

LU RAE: *(Without stopping)* Sorry, I'm late!

SHAUNELLE: LU RAE!!!

(The girl stops on a dime and returns. SHAUNELLE continues...)

SHAUNELLE: I changed my mind.

LU RAE: *(Lightly)* Good idea, Mom. You needed a new one.

SHAUNELLE: I think you should be aboard for this getaway.

LU RAE: Hot damn! I love excitement.

SHAUNELLE: You head up t'the kootch. Only double-back when yer free. Then go get the car an' head down t'the gas station yonder. *(Pointing off)* Point the car t'the interstate headed north an' hit the horn.

LU RAE: You bet! *(Starts off)*

SHAUNELLE: LU RAE! Can't you gimmee a goodbye kiss?

LU RAE: I won't be gone but fer a few minutes, Shaunelle. *(She's gone)*

SHAUNELLE: *(Quietly to herself)* Can't you call me "Momma"?

(RICKY emerges. SHAUNELLE addresses him...)

SHAUNELLE: That's the last we'll see of her.

RICKY: She ain't got the slightest idea of what we're up to.

SHAUNELLE: Well, one more rehearsal. Then we load up fer the real McCoy.

RICKY: Ya never got that call from God?

SHAUNELLE: He never came through.

RICKY: He never does.

SHAUNELLE: Gimmee a, "Say, Officer Beazley..."

RICKY: *(Quivering)* S-s-say, Officer Beazley...

SHAUNELLE: Now, gimmee the gun.

(He does so. She continues...)

SHAUNELLE: Atta boy, don't be nervous. *(To the invisible BEAZLEY)* Meetcher match, Macho Man! BANG! *(Click)* Then the kiss.

(They kiss briefly.)

SHAUNELLE: Hey, what's that? Ya call that a kiss?

RICKY: I'm savin' up fer the real thing.

SHAUNELLE: Ricky, today's our rainy day, so t'speak. Now, the gun t' my head.

RICKY: *(The gun to SHAUNELLE's head)* B-B-Bang. *(Click)*

SHAUNELLE: *(Falls, then looking up at him...)* The gun t'your head. *(Pause)* Go ahead!

RICKY: I c-c-can't.

SHAUNELLE: Now, squeeze...squeeze...c'mon, ya almost got it.

RICKY: Ba—... *(Click)* Ba... Ba...

SHAUNELLE: Forget it. Just keel over.

(RICKY falls. SHAUNELLE continues...)

SHAUNELLE: Now, I'll load 'er up. You're too nervous. *(She turns her back and loads the two bullets.)* You still with me, boy?

RICKY: S-S-Sure. Where else w-w-would I be?

SHAUNELLE: Ya sound like yer hankerin' t' fly the coop.

RICKY: W-W-What gives ya that n-n-notion?

SHAUNELLE: John Wayne woulda faced death right inna eye. Gregory Peck...Jimmy Cagney...

RICKY: *(Half-crying)* Jee-zusssssss

SHAUNELLE: Shhhhh. Here he comes.

RICKY: W-W-Where?

SHAUNELLE: Big as life an' dead ahead.

(RICKY winces. SHAUNELLE rephrases...)

SHAUNELLE: Sorry, *straight* ahead. Let's duck outta sight 'til he gets a few yards closer... How ya feelin'?

(They duck away though not out of sight.)

RICKY: I'm c-c-cool as a cu-cu-cu-

SHAUNELLE: *(Ignoring him)* Little ways more.

(BEAZLEY enters with fresh-picked flowers and in a mellow mood.)

BEAZLEY: *(Singing)* You're a queen, Shaun. Never mean, Shaun. You melt the snow and turn the winters green, Shaun.

SHAUNELLE: *(Whispering)* Let's do it!

(SHAUNELLE steps out from the shadows. RICKY—paralyzed with fright— does not. SHAUNELLE is unseen by BEAZLEY.)

RICKY: *(Trying to deliver his one and only line)* S-S-S-S-

SHAUNELLE: *(Whispering angrily at him)* "Sheriff Beazley!"

(Nothing from RICKY but panic)

(SHAUNELLE whispers lividly...)

SHAUNELLE: Say it!

(RICKY delivers a silent scream. SHAUNELLE turns the gun on RICKY's head.)

RICKY: *(High-pitched)* Say, Sheriff Beazley.

BEAZLEY: *(Alerted by the sound but seeing only SHAUNELLE)* Why, if it ain't my little flower-face. Ready to take up where we left off last year?

SHAUNELLE: Meetcher match, Macho Man!

(She has the gun leveled at his groin. He panics and defenses.)

BEAZLEY: No, no, Shaun. Let's talk this—

SHAUNELLE: Never fear, Merle. I'd never blow away yer puny manhood.

BEAZLEY: *(Relaxing and approaching)* You're pullin' my leg. Hey, that's a start. How 'bout a kiss fer ole Merlekins. Then some home cookin' an' some... recreational—

(She raises the gun to his heart. He throws the flowers in her face and goes for his own gun but she plugs him. RICKY goes wide-eyed as BEAZLEY grabs futilely for SHAUNELLE.)

BEAZLEY: *(Mortally wounded)* You bitch! I shoulda plugged you last year when I was through with ya. No more...Mister...Nice Guy.

(He expires.)

(SHAUNELLE turns to semi-hysterical RICKY.)

SHAUNELLE: Now, kiss me.

(She kisses him passionately. He responds. She tucks the gun into his hand.)

RICKY: I'm aroused. Can we take a short break fer a quickie?

SHAUNELLE: I'm ready. Fire!

RICKY: N-N-No witnesses. We can make a run fer it.

SHAUNELLE: *(Menacing)* Look, if you freeze now, I'll kill ya just like I killed him.

(She lifts the gun in his hand to her head.)

RICKY: Wouldn't put it past ya. Yer a woman of her word.

SHAUNELLE: C'mon, yer shakin' like a leaf. Ready...aim...FIRE!

(RICKY is a quivering wreck. SHAUNELLE becomes hysterical.)

SHAUNELLE: DAMMIT RICKY, WHY CAN'T YOU FACE UP TO LIFE'S EVERYDAY OBLIGATIONS??? WHY I EVER FELL FER A POLECAT LIKE YOU-

(Unnerved, he fires and SHAUNELLE collapses atop BEAZLEY.)

RICKY: *(Simultaneous with the firing)* PIPE DOWN, WILL YA! *(A long pause as the shock of recognition sets in)* Oh, my God. Oh, looky here. I gone an' went

an' done it. My poor Shaunelle. (*He kneels and takes her in his arms.*)
Well, no turnin' back. Gotta honor my promise. (*Raising the gun to his head*) W-W-Well, goodbye cruel world. Cruel as y' are, I was j-j-just startin' t-t-t' warm up t' ya. Here goes. R-R-Ready...aim...woe is me...FIRE!
(*Click. Nonetheless, he collapses as if he'd been shot. He lies still for a long moment. Then, without moving...*) This must be the easiest way t'go. I never felt a thing.
(*Slowly, he becomes aware that he's alive. He touches his temple and exclaims...*) I'm alive!!! I can't have this!!! (*He fires again. Click. Again. Click. He desperately examines the gun, exploring the chamber and discovering...*) There ain't no bullets in here! (*He leaps up and rushes to retrieve the bullet box. Nothing. He searches the ground and the truth starts to dawn on him as he mutters...*) One fer him...one fer her... What about me? WHAT ABOUT ME, SHAUN??? (*Scrambling to her and in her face...*) You ain't gettin' away with this. I'll use a knife. I'll turn on the oven. I can't live without you. THERE'S NO REASON FOR LIVIN' WITHOUT YOU!!!

(*As he's about to rush into the trailer, a car pulls up offstage and a horn sounds.*)

LU RAE: (*Off*) LET'S GET MOVIN'!

RICKY: (*Beat. His expression changes as he points to himself*) Me? (*To himself*) On second thought...

(*The horn sounds again. He looks to* SHAUNELLE *and confesses...*)

RICKY: I tried, baby. I give it my all. But you must know that if an execution fails, I'm offa the hook. Prison-wise, at least. An' I gotta hunch you set this up. So, I'll hafta take a raincheck. Lu Rae needs lookin' after. That's what you musta had in mind. Given her behavior, I might wish sometimes I could trade places with ya. (*He kneels and inserts the gun in her hand.*) I'm doin' this so I'm offa the hook. I know you wouldn't want me t'go back t'jail. I mean, I arready served time fer ya. (*Standing*) Well, gotta get movin'. I truly loved ya, Shaunelle. Always will. Maybe not like The Three-Eyed-Man loves The Bearded Lady... But in my own way.

(*The car horn sounds ceaselessly. He starts off angrily, yelling...*)

RICKY: I'M COMIN'! I'M COMIN'! DON'T YOU FIGGER I'M UNDER YER THUMB. I'M TURNIN OVER A NEW LEAF...BE WEARIN' MY BUTT-KICKIN' BOOTIES, NOW. RICKY RUANE'S HIS OWN MAN, NOW.

(*We hear* LU RAE *laugh uproariously from the short distance.*)

(*The calliope music comes up and the lights start to fade as* RICKY *starts off muttering to himself...*)

RICKY: I swear, like step-momma, like step-daughter!

(*Lights fade out on the two bodies as* RICKY *exits.*)

END OF PLAY

SHOOTERS

For support with the development of SHOOTERS, thanks to New Dramatists.

SHOOTERS premiered at Focus Theatre, Dublin, Ireland by PurpleHeart Theatre Company (Stewart Roche, Artistic Director; Tana French, Managing Director) in November, 2005. The cast and creative contributors were:

LOU . . . . .Stewart Roche
BARRY . . . . Dermot Magennis
ARLENE . . . . Mary Kelly
MOLLY . . . . Tana French

Director . . . . John O'Brien
Fight director . . . . .Paul Burke
Designer . . . . Martin Cahill
Lighting designer . . . . Simon Maxwell
Costume designer . . . . .Donna Geraghty
Sound design & original music . . . . .David Gillespie
Graphic design . . . . Keith Hobson
Photography . . . . .Lesley Conroy
Press & P R . . . . Stewart Roche & Tana French
Set construction . . . . Martin Cahill
Printing . . . . Direct Print

SHOOTERS had its American premiere at BacklotArts Theater (Mark Marvell, Executive Director), Sarasota FL in January 2006. The cast and creative contributors were:

LOU .... Steve Grabo
BARRY .... Jim McGinnis
ARLENE .... Seva Anthony
MOLLY .... Margret Taylor

Director .... Jack Gilhooley
Assistant director .... Thomas Griffin
Stage manager/Technical director .... Richard B Pell

to Jo

PART ONE: BAD BOYS

CHARACTERS & SETTING

LOU, *a young killer though he's well-educated, sophisticated and somewhat of the manner born. He's usually well-spoken but on occasion he's capable of playing the hood—especially over the phone with the boss—and he sort of enjoys it.*

BARRY, LOU'*s partner in crime. A very plain, undemonstrative young man who excels only at killing. But lately—after an occupational brush with death—he's been undergoing a transition and he's lost his heart for his art.*

Time: The present

Place: A low-rent, shabbily-furnished Brighton Beach (Brooklyn) apartment living room. It in no way reflects the income of the pair which is considerable since they're at the top of their game.

There's a doorway leading outside, a door (leading to an offstage bedroom) and a window. There's a laptop computer and a map of the N Y C area with pins protruding.

Suggested music: I'm Just a Bad Boy *by The Jive Bombers, 1957, or* Bad Boy *by Eric Clapton (Derek and The Dominoes), circa 1980. There are others songs with the same title.*

Scene One

(LOU *is on the phone. He's dressed tastefully if one doesn't count the shoulder holster. He certainly sounds every bit the professional hit man...until he hangs up.*)

(BARRY *is hidden behind the tabloid* N Y Post *[headline: GANGLAND WIPEOUT]. He is morose and he's plainly attired. He too, is armed with a gun in a shoulder holster. He certainly doesn't exhibit his partner's occupational enthusiasm.*)

LOU: (*Into the phone, very macho*) Yeah, gotcha boss... Nah, he was an easy hit. But unique. A Muslim. A first for us, far as I know. He tried to use it as leverage. (*Beat*) Huh?... "Leverage." Like a bargaining chip. He said, (*Accented*) "Please sir, I'm a devout Muslim." Like, *that's* gonna cut some ice with me. I replied, "Well, I am a Christian, Abdul. That means I shoot you before you shoot me. You guys have us targeted. Like we're devils...evil incarnate.

(BARRY *lowers his paper, stares, then he re-reads.*)

LOU: "So I better get you before you get me." Then I plugged him. Only not in the head. In the gut. For 9-11. But also, to witness this guy's departure if he's so devout. Then Barry pops up, "Show us your inner peace now, buddy."

BARRY: (*Irritated, he lowers the paper*) Did not! (*He walks around the room to let off steam.*)

LOU: He says, "You see those sixty virgins on the horizon, Abdul?"

(BARRY *threatens unintimidated* LOU *with a gesture.*)

LOU: You know Barry, boss. Always jokin' around with the victim. Like a little kid playin' with his food. No sappy sentiments from this boy. A cold-hearted son-of-a-bitch, Barry is.

BARRY: Maybe not, Lou. Maybe I've changed.

LOU: (*Ignoring him*) Omar The Tentmaker is rollin' around onna ground an' beggin' for mercy. Just like alla the rest of 'em, religious or not. Barry says, "You wanna say an Act of Contrition, Abdul? You go right to Heaven. With Jesus." Barry was an altar boy as a kid. (*Emphatically into the phone*) *An altar boy*... (*To* BARRY, *quietly imitating a Russian accent*) "Vhat's an altar boy?"

(BARRY *shrugs him off and* LOU *reverts to the phone.*)

LOU: Never mind. Lemmee just say it left an impression on Barr. So much so that he kneels over Omar and leads him in prayer.

(BARRY *is increasingly angry at the bogus reporting. He seethes at amused* LOU *who continues in mock-prayer...*)

LOU: "Hail Mary, full of grace..." *(To* BARRY*)* What comes after that, Barr? *(To the phone after Barry's silence)* Yeah, yeah, I'm gettin' to it, Boss. I just figured you'd like a detailed report...y' know, your money's worth. Arright, so devout Mr. Omar stops snivilin' an' bawlin' just long enough to give Barry the finger. So much for this guy's piety. "Uh-oh", says I. The ole dirty digit. *(He raises his middle finger.)* Well, that made Barry's day. BANG! *(He retracts the finger.)* Off with the ole fingeroo. Then...BANG! again. Off with Abdul... Huh?. Omar, Abdul, what's the diff? Boss, we got the right dude. The turban guy.

(BARRY *keeps seething but* LOU *is on a roll.*)

LOU: Barry's one mean motha. He loves you, Boss. But don't ever give Barry the ole fingeroo fongool. He just goes batshit...

BARRY: *(Befuddled, pretty much to himself)* "Fingeroo fongool." Where does he pick up...

LOU: *(Into the phone)* Yeah, I gotcha. New Jersey, tomorrow.

BARRY: *(Suddenly engaged)* New Jersey? That's an extra two thousand dollars.

LOU: *(Timidly into the phone)* Begging your pardon, Boss... That's an extra two thousand dollars. *(Beat...To* BARRY*)* He says, "Keel him here, dump him in New Jersey."

BARRY: That's even more. We'll be wanted in two states.

LOU: *(Into the phone)* Two grand extra, Boss... *(Beat, then to* BARRY *imitating The Boss)* "A keel in New Jersey should not be extra. Eet's a common t'ing over dere."

BARRY: Non-negotiable.

LOU: Hold on, Barry... In that case, The Boss says he wants the hit on the guy's front porch. In New Jersey.

BARRY: What county?

LOU: *(To* BARRY*)* What county???

BARRY: Look, I'm a pro. *(Indicating the map)* I've researched. Mercer County...rich people. Paranoids. The cops are paid to hunt us down. But Camden County...another slaying. *(Pseudo-yawning)* Ho-hum.

LOU: I'd have never thought of that. You're a genius, Barr. *(Into the phone with reluctance)* What county? *(He recoils from The Boss's explosion. To*

Barry...*)* He says he doesn't know counties. They don't have counties in Russia.

Barry: *(Contemptuously)* Right, they have gulags.

Lou: *(He extends the phone, a hand over the receiver)* He wants to talk to you.

Barry: You're such a pussy.

Lou: *(Threatening to go for his gun)* I'm a pussy??? I have to cover for you when you don't do the job! And I can't piss The Boss off. He's a killer.

Barry: What're we, chopped liver?

(He takes the phone. Lou *looks out the window, surveying the neighborhood. Then he starts energetically cleaning his gun.)*

Barry: Barry here, Boss... A front porch job is more expensive, even. If the family sees it, that's a real problem... A problem for us. We are not totally devoid of sensitivity. It's also a problem since kids remember. In ten...twenty years they could hunt down their father's killer. Y'know, if they're really pissed...unforgiving.

Lou: Let bygones be bygones. That's my motto.

Barry: Most of the guys we stiffen, their families don't care. But a vengeful kid, he could shoot me on *my* front porch years from now. It's a vicious circle... *(Reacting to The Boss)* I *could* have a front porch by then! A wife and kids. God knows, I won't be in this dump much— "Economy job"? Y'mean a hit with no extras? That's not like you to go tourist, Boss. You wouldn't drive a car with no extras... Just a flat ten grand? ...Gotcha, money's tight. *(To* Lou, *grinning)* He's sending Natasha home.... Find a nice Russian boy...get married.

(They quietly break up over this as Lou *mimes ugly, heavy-set Natasha, and* Barry *continues.)*

Barry: Well y'know, outta the crime mainstream we could lowball you. Upstate, maybe. Poughkeepsie, for instance, we could do a cheap wipeout.

Lou: I'd shoot *myself* before I'd go to Poughkeepsie.

*(*Lou *will put on a black silk shirt and a white tie. He'll transfer his shoulder holster. He'll check himself out in a mirror [visible or otherwise]).*

Barry: *(Into the phone.)* Because it's safer. Safer for us. It's never safe for the mark. It's fatal. That's as unsafe as you can get. Isn't that the point? *(He indicates his frustration with the argumentative boss.)* You could pop a guy at twelve noon in Poughkeepsie. On Main Street. They've got their middle-class, ordered lives. Kids in school. Church on Sunday. Stool pigeons in Witness Protection move there it's so square. Even local cops, they get an emergency call they do a one-eighty for Kerhonksin. In hopes that the problem resolves itself.

LOU: To die in Poughkeepsie would be escape. To die in Kerhonksin would be redundant.

BARRY: *(Into the phone)* O K, thirteen thousand. The entire package. *(Gesturing for* LOU *to write)* 423 Elmcrest Drive, Edison, New Jersey... What do I want with the phone number? He might have one of those gizmos. They trace the call. That's one of the problems with this country. There's no level playing field for shooters, anymore.
Eight o'clock. A M or P M?
 Whoaaaa! P M's overtime...O K, O K, I gave you a quote. Never mind the O T. This is a favor. I won't forget the flowers in January when I was in the hospital. You're a sensitive guy. Y' know, to a point. My own family didn't even visit. Didn't send a fuckin' card, even. Nothing...just cause I got hurt.

LOU: Shot! Occupational hazard.

BARRY: Boss, if I wanted to dispatch my family I could do it myself. Death isn't the answer to everything. *(Beat)* I couldn't be better. Thanks for asking. God forbid you should ever get shot. Brooklyn Hospital has a terrific trauma unit.

LOU: *(Off-handedly)* Lotta trauma in Brooklyn.

BARRY: Amazing what modern medicine can do. Right. Caio. *(Hanging up, then to* LOU, *emphatically)* Why that bullshit about last night?

LOU: I gotta cover your ass. Keep peace in the family.

BARRY: *You* did all the dirty work.

LOU: I've done all the dirty work since January.

BARRY: Well...I'm in recuperation.

LOU: Bullshit! You've been leading a full life...well, for *you* it's a full life.

BARRY: Psychological recuperation. I'm conflicted.

LOU: Just cause a hit fired back?

BARRY: Well yeah, matter-of-fact.

LOU: So why were you just cutting the next deal with Ivan The Terrible? *(Pointing to the phone)*

BARRY: I'm cool to killing. I'm hot for dough. It doesn't take two guys to squeeze off a shot. A single slug to the back of the head. That's how you did it last night, huh?

LOU: Yeah. But I felt obligated to say that you were aboard. Like you were a player.

BARRY: A "player"? Some game.

LOU: Everything's "spin", nowadays. I'm saving your job by bullshitting the boss. Man, you used to love this line of work.

BARRY: It was easy. I fantasized each guy as my abusive father.

LOU: What about when we shot Lola Carpenter?

BARRY: She was my abusive mother. But after I killed off enough pseudo-parents I lost my motivation.

LOU: I don't believe that. Just now, you were motivated on the phone. It's my fault. When you got out of the hospital, I should've put you right back to work.

BARRY: *(Fraternally)* You've got a good heart, Lou. Like a brother to me.

LOU: Didn't I bring Shirley in to nurse you?

BARRY: I'm grateful. You're lucky. A beautiful wife who's a nurse. Someday—God forbid—you should get plugged, you've got Shirley.

LOU: I don't intend to get plugged. You were careless.

BARRY: Not careless. I tried to put some pizzaz into things. Rub-outs had been getting monotonous. Lethargy can be a killer. No pun intended. I had developed the attitude that humanity was nothing more than worm chow.

LOU: Well, it is. And it's circular. We eat birds, birds eat worms, worms eat us.

BARRY: So much for God's beautiful master plan.

LOU: You *let* it get boring. Assassination should never be a slam dunk. *You just don't challenge a mark to a quick draw contest!!!*

BARRY: I wanted to give him a fighting chance, albeit slight.

LOU: WHY???

BARRY: *(Sheepishly)* I still won.

LOU: At a steep, steep price.

BARRY: *(Proudly)* I hit him between the eyes.

LOU: He hit you in the chest. And you weren't wearing your bullet-proof vest.

BARRY: It makes me perspire.

LOU: It nearly made you *ex*pire. You'd rather die than sweat?

BARRY: Nowadays, I wanna live and *not* sweat.

LOU: But you still wanna be on the payroll? While I put my life on the line?

BARRY: You never put your life on the line, Lou! You wait 'til the mark lets his guard down...gets loaded, maybe. Then you put a bullet through his head...from behind, I might add.

LOU: Or *her head.*

BARRY: Lola was an accident. A one-and-only experience. She had the misfortune to look like Mommy.

LOU: Well, I don't know how much longer I can work alone. You're my decoy. I can't get a bead on a mark unless they're distracted. And that's your specialty. Nobody does it like you, Barry. When we skunked that guy, Teborian you learned Armenian.

BARRY: *(Smiles modestly but proudly)* Ah, the rudiments was all.

LOU: You promise them heroin from Turkey if they'll meet you in the alley.

BARRY: I promise 'em porn stars.

LOU: Courtside seats for the Knicks and Lakers.

BARRY: Anything to get their guard down. But I just don't wanna be on-site anymore.

LOU: What's that mean? You want out??? How will you live on your librarian's salary?

BARRY: I lived on it before. I don't want to witness the shootings. I want to plan them.

LOU: WELL, DOESN'T EVERYONE???

(Silence. Things calm down, then...)

BARRY: Look Lou, the fact is...well, I've gotten very good on the internet. Y'know, during my recuperation.

LOU: You couldn't have lost the aptitude. I mean, shooting is like riding a bike.

BARRY: *(Incredulously)* What???

LOU: *(Demonstrating)* Or like line dancing.

BARRY: Like line dancing???

LOU: Once you've done it for awhile, you don't lose the aptitude.

BARRY: Once you've been shot you do!!! *(Subsiding)* I'll be perfectly content to help you. But as a consultant.

LOU: Everybody's a fuckin' consultant, nowadays. Doesn't anyone work anymore?

BARRY: I can map out your route...trace the cop's whereabouts...

LOU: You can do all that on the computer?

BARRY: Well...I can venture an educated guess. You wanna beer?

LOU: *(Shrugs)* We're on call.

BARRY: For tomorrow. He won't tap us tonight.

(BARRY *exits.* LOU *puts on a light-colored sportcoat that makes him look very much the hood. He likes what he sees in the mirror as he adjusts his holster under his armpit then puts on dark sunglasses.* BARRY *returns with two beers.)*

LOU: This is a good holster. Myriad hours under my armpit and it still smells like leather.

(BARRY *stares at* LOU *in semi-disbelief. Then they sit and drink and reflect.)*

LOU: Forget your "educated guess". Assassination is not a guessing game. Computers won't do. So I guess I'll need a new partner. Years of savvy...pissed away. You can't recruit today's kids. They just grab a gun and blaze away.

BARRY: Which is why they don't last very long.

LOU: The boss likes guys like us. Mature...responsible. And non-goombahs.

BARRY: We have standards. Especially you, Lou.

LOU: Damn right. This occupation has required a major adjustment for me. A sort of monkish devotion.

BARRY: Well, I dunno if monks are devoted to assass—

LOU: Barry, a figure of speech. I was not born into crime.

BARRY: I know. I heard. Me neither.

LOU: I'm well-educated...a cultured family.

BARRY: C'mon, Lou. I met your father. A born killer.

LOU: A lawyer. Maybe that's where I got it. This is not something that I learned at Yale. I was on a steady course. Dean's List...on occasion. An M B A.

BARRY: *(Slight weariness)* Ivy League.

LOU: I mixed well. Communicated. Debutantes targeted me.

BARRY: Me, too. Well, ...one debutante. Sorta.

LOU: I was always invited back.

BARRY: To where?

LOU: To wherever I'd been. I observed my contemporaries. They were on the right track, socially...occupationally.

BARRY: But on the wrong train, huh?

LOU: No. I was on the wrong train.

BARRY: I get what you mean, Lou. There comes a time when conformity becomes a burden.

LOU: Outlaws, Barry. You and me.

BARRY: Some people are born into it. Others—

LOU: —have it thrust upon them.

(They smile at one another.)

BARRY: Hard to explain.

LOU: Well, we're lone wolves.

(Quietly howling, wolf-like, BARRY joins in.)

BARRY: It's hard to maintain relationships.

LOU: People don't understand.

BARRY: Shirley doesn't.

LOU: *(Surprised)* Huh?

BARRY: Shirley. Your wife.

LOU: I know who my wife is.

BARRY: Sure you do.

LOU: She's been talking to you?

BARRY: *(Shrugging innocently)* We converse.

LOU: About us?

BARRY: You...and me?

LOU: Me and her.

BARRY: She's not happy.

LOU: She told you this?

BARRY: How would she be happy? She's a sensitive girl.

LOU: She doesn't turn back the do-re-mi.

BARRY: It's not about money.

LOU: Sez you. What's it about, then?

BARRY: You have to ask?

LOU: She has to tell *you*?

BARRY: I'm a friend.

LOU: Of hers?

BARRY: Of both of you.

LOU: Look Barr, what attracted her to me is what attracted the boss.

BARRY: *(Surprised)* The boss is gay?

LOU: No, no. They both wanted an All-American clean-cut type.

BARRY: The Russian mob is different. And it's paid off.

LOU: They don't even hire themselves.

BARRY: They're afraid of themselves.

LOU: When I interviewed, I convinced them. I learned marksmanship by skeet shooting. From clay pigeons to stool pigeons. An easy transition.

BARRY: Ruskies aren't tradition-bound.

LOU: At my last college reunion I figured I earned in the top two percentile.

BARRY: Growing up, I never thought I'd be working for Russians.

LOU: I never thought I'd be working for gangsters.

BARRY: You worked for gangsters on Wall Street.

LOU: *(Miming a marksman)* A simple trip to the shooting range... my whole life changed.

BARRY: Yeah, that's where they recruited me. My income sure shot up.

LOU: *(Looking around the shabby room)* Yeah, but we can't spend it.

BARRY: *(Mimicking the boss)* "I want no osten...osten-vatchamacallit."

LOU: A sure-fire tip-off to the feds.

BARRY: This dump smacks of poverty.

LOU: It's just our base of operations.

BARRY: *(Checking himself in the mirror)* I'll never stand out in a crowd.

LOU: No way. Even in a suit you look like a librarian...who's been downsized.

BARRY: *(Concerned)* So that outfit you're wearing, Lou...a pinky-ring short of the underworld. The Boss wouldn't approve.

LOU: It's something I've got to do once in a while. Busman's holiday. *(Peering out the window)* Those punks on the corner...

BARRY: Wannabees.

LOU: They'd diss me when I'd walk by in a suit. Like I was some sort of wuss.

BARRY: Not by the notches on your gun.

LOU: They don't sneer now. Clothes make the man, Barr. Still, I'd like to waste a couple of those—

BARRY: For free???

(LOU *shrugs his shoulders.*)

BARRY: Hey, you're a professional. Where's your pride? Your dignity? You can't just waste some kids without compensation.

LOU: True. I have a code of ethics. (*Heading off evasively*) Well, I'm goin' out.

BARRY: Where do you go?

LOU: I walk. You know I'm a great walker. All over Brighton...down to Coney. I reflect on what Brooklyn used to be.

BARRY: Y'mean, back when The Dodgers—

LOU: No, way back.

BARRY: Y'mean, Walt Whitman?

LOU: (*Pseudo-philosophical and to the window*) I mean when it was a wilderness. And the natives...or the early settlers would look across the river. They'd marvel at their great good fortune knowing that Manhattan would some day bloat...then putrify. Those Colonial dreamers must have felt blessed by the bounty that was Brooklyn...the rustic tranquility...the New World's Garden of Eden. But spared the same dark fate by the merciful forewarning of the Old Testament.

BARRY: Babes, huh?

LOU: Wha...?

BARRY: Eve, in particular. Y'know, the Garden of Eden. In the Old Testament.

LOU: I dunno why you always focus on women.

BARRY: You brought it up.

LOU: I was waxing.

BARRY: Huh?

LOU: Philosophical.

(*They both pause and ponder.*)

BARRY: I thought you waxed *poetic.*

LOU: Not me.

BARRY: Geez, it's hard to think of this neighborhood *sans* sleaze.

LOU: Well, there's always been sleaze.

BARRY: Always will be.

LOU: Or else we'd be out of work.

BARRY: *(Toasting)* Hail, sleaze!

(They click glasses in camaraderie, two pals at ease with themselves and with the world.)

LOU: You said it, buddy.

BARRY: What a happy accident.

LOU: Y'mean, you and me...teaming up?

BARRY: Serendipitous.

LOU: There are very few hitmen who could use that word. And fewer who'd understand it.

BARRY: We're like those colonial beneficiaries of the dream.

LOU: You got a bit of Whitman in you, Barr.

BARRY: *(Staring at him, somewhat sternly)* Whitman *the poet*, you mean?

LOU: Of course. Whataya think?

BARRY: *(Beat, then concerned)* My sister says you've been in to see her.

LOU: *(Innocently)* Lily?

BARRY: Lori! You know her name, Lou. Don't bullshit me, buddy.

LOU: So I stopped in. So what?

BARRY: You're married.

LOU: Sooooo...? I'm not hustlin' the girl, Barr. I'm not hittin' on her.

BARRY: Better you do your hittin' for the boss. Or I might get rejuvenated.

(In an instant LOU whips out his gun and overpowers BARRY with the weapon at his frightened partner's neck.)

LOU: I could do some free-lance hitting!!! Spontaneous...but efficient.

BARRY: Hey, ole buddy...your paranoia's getting the best of you.

LOU: Lori's a pal, that's all. As I thought I was.

BARRY: Of her or of me?

LOU: *(Relaxing)* Of the both of you.

BARRY: You're a pal of mine, Lou. Big time.

(LOU *withdraws, putting away the gun.*)

BARRY: But keep away from Lori.

LOU: Keep Lori away *from me,* then !!!

BARRY: I just don't want her...well...

LOU: Yeah? Spit it out!

BARRY: I don't want my sister running around with a killer.

LOU: That's coming from *you*??? I think Lori's old enough to choose her own company. If you're so pure, why not turn yourself in?

BARRY: Don't wish for that, Lou. I'd have to rat you out.

(LOU *goes for his gun but* BARRY *beats him to it by drawing a bead.* LOU *is guarded as he tries diplomacy.*)

LOU: I thought you were through with killing?

BARRY: Not quite. You *could* be my swan song, amigo.

LOU: I know you, Barry. It's not gonna happen.

BARRY: Just stay away from Lori.

LOU: No skin off my ass.

BARRY: She's a good kid. I just wanna keep her clean.

LOU: Wait a reality-check minute, here. You know what she does for a living.

BARRY: *(Evasively)* She's a...an actress.

LOU: Worse, even! She's a stripper.

BARRY: That's not her vocation.

LOU: Right, it just pays the bills. Including her acting classes...her cottage upstate.

BARRY: Hey, what do you know about her cottage upsta—

LOU: Only, other actresses wait tables.

BARRY: Lori's got attributes.

LOU: Why pick on me? Hundreds of guys go to the Pussycat just to look at Lori.

BARRY: They're not hitmen.

LOU: *(Shrugs)* A couple, maybe.

BARRY: How can you tell?

LOU: Y' know, body language.

BARRY: We have our own body language?

LOU: Yeah. Y' know, from hidden weapons. We tend to hunch.

(They go through a mini-ritual of "hunching". LOU crosses and BARRY follows [hunch]. Then...)

BARRY: Anyway, she's leaving the Pussycat. She opens in a play next month.

LOU: I know. We're running lines.

BARRY: COCAINE???

LOU: No, no. I'm helping her memorize

BARRY: Lines?

LOU: What d'ya think, *The Lord's Prayer*?

BARRY: She already knows *The Lord's Prayer*. Does she keep her clothes on?

LOU: Certainly.

BARRY: I don't like it.

LOU: That she keeps her clothes on?

BARRY: That she's with you.

LOU: You told me. Nonetheless, I'm going out.

BARRY: When will you be back?

LOU: What're you, my mother?

BARRY: "Who're you", Lou. I should think that a Yale grad would know the proper usage.

LOU: I'll be late. *Very* late. I'm feeling very contemplative. I may even walk to Manhattan.

BARRY: Leave the gun.

LOU: I *need* the gun. Walking the streets of Brooklyn, in the dead of night...

BARRY: Dressed like that, you invite the cops.

LOU: Well...maybe. *(He leaves his gun.)* I feel naked.

BARRY: That doesn't mean you have anything in common with my sister.

LOU: If you don't like your sister's stripping then throw some dough her way. *(He exits the apartment.)*

(BARRY looks at the door for a long moment then he exits to the kitchen. He quickly returns with a bottle of wine and two glasses. He looks out the window at departing LOU. Then he looks at the telephone. He crosses, picks it up and starts to dial.)

(Blackout)

Scene Two

(The next morning)

(The empty bottle of wine on the table and the two glasses. One seems to have lipstick stains.)

(LOU enters. He's had a long evening. He puts his gun on the table. He looks at the glasses and the bottle. He picks up the lipstick-stained glass, examines it carefully and the licks the lipstick. He reacts to the taste...savors...licks again, then grimaces. BARRY enters from the bedroom in his pajamas. He has just awakened but wears his gun and holster.)

LOU: I know this lipstick.

(He glares at BARRY then darts past him and into the bedroom.)

(In a minor panic, BARRY empties LOU's gun of the ammo then reinserts it in the shoulder holster on the table.)

LOU: *(Off)* Where is she?

BARRY: She came here looking for you.

LOU: *(Re-entering)* That's no reason for having a party.

BARRY: A glass of wine is not a party.

LOU: A *bottle!*

BARRY: We talked.

LOU: I'm sure.

BARRY: Shirley isn't happy, Lou.

LOU: Tell me about it. Sitting in a fleabag apartment drinking cheap wine with a deadbeat killer...who'd be happy?

BARRY: Now just one minute there...

LOU: *(Examining the bottle)* How far she has fallen. Time was she'd never drink this piss.

BARRY: She told me about your halcyon days.

LOU: *(Staring at LOU)* We never had halcyon days. We may have been devoted to one another. But we didn't spend dreamy nights in one another's arms. Our romance was not heaven-sent. It was touch-and-go...helter-skelter.

BARRY: That was before you started shooting people?

LOU: Of course it was. Back when we were poor as church mice.

BARRY: I think it's *"quiet* as church—"

LOU: Who used that word "halcyon"?

BARRY: Lots have used it, I guess. Nobody has a monop—

LOU: Between you and Shirley? Who said "halcyon"?

BARRY: I don't remember. Maybe neither of us.

LOU: Neither??? Well, why am I arguing semantics, then?

BARRY: Beats me. Shirley said your relationship was frenetic.

LOU: "Frenetic"? She said that?

BARRY: No. I paraphrased.

LOU: *(Ponders, then...)* Well, she's too subjective.

BARRY: But it's right from the horse's mouth.

LOU: It wasn't that bad.

BARRY: She had doubts about marrying you.

LOU: I did her a favor.

(LOU is speechless, then indicating the bottle...)

LOU: What's in this rotgut?
How could she— ...I mean, you're a stranger...practically.

BARRY: "A stranger"? She saved my life.

LOU: The doctors saved your life.

BARRY: She nursed me back to health.

LOU: Don't assume it was personal. She gets off on that Florence Nightingale shtick.

BARRY: "Florence Nightingale shtick"???

LOU: She's a nurse. Y'know, by training.

BARRY: Certainly I know.

LOU: It's a rush for her.

BARRY: Well, maybe more people should "rush" like that. Instead of drugging, for instance.

LOU: I don't drug.

BARRY: God, you're insecure. I was drawing an example.

LOU: When she'd heard you'd been shot, she said, *(Imitating satirically)* "Poor Barry, I should help him. He has no family."

BARRY: I have a family.

LOU: They've disavowed you. Except for your sister.

BARRY: They've disavowed *her, too*. But we don't care. We're the only ones who've made anything of themselves. The rest of out family aspires to dysfunction.

LOU: I said, "Shirley, you've got two kids to raise. Barry's gonna be fine."

BARRY: Of yeah, about your kids—

(LOU goes semi-ballistic.)

LOU: What about my kids??? What did she tell you??? *My* kids are *my* business!!!

BARRY: Yours and Shirley's.

LOU: So, what did she tell you?

BARRY: That they miss you very much.

LOU: *(Mellowing)* Yeah? That's nice. I'll make it up to them. This is a demanding job. Like athletics.

BARRY: Athletics? We play chess. That's it.

LOU: We have a short shelf life. And it's a demanding job. On call in this apartment... Waiting for our next assignment. But private schools are expensive...summers in Europe...Christmas in Aspen.

BARRY: Aspen no longer does it for Shirley.

LOU: *(Staring at him)* It's come to this? Confiding in you about our marriage.

BARRY: We're friends. When I was dying, I confided in her.

LOU: You were never dying.

BARRY: I thought I was.

LOU: You two shared intimacies?

BARRY: Confidences. I couldn't be intimate with a bullet in my chest.

LOU: You could. Shirley's long since abandoned the missionary position.

BARRY: I simply told her about my brutal childhood.

LOU: She's a sucker for cheap melodrama. A real bleeding heart. *(Smiles)* No pun intended.

BARRY: Hey, my inner turmoil is not the result of cheap melo—

LOU: You sure know how to push her button. So how far has it gone with you two?

BARRY: I didn't get to her button, if that's what—

LOU: Watch it, Barry!

BARRY: Hey Lou...easy, huh? Man, your defensiveness knows no bounds. We're friends, that's all. I do not have sex with a friend's wife. Especially when his kids are involved.

LOU: IN SEX???

BARRY: OF COURSE NOT!!! There's no sex. I told Shirley I'm not interested in a woman with two kids.

LOU: I'd say that's admirable of you. Except you're only concerned with your own comfort. You don't want the responsibility of another's children.

BARRY: Shirley shared the wine, then left. She wanted to wait for you but I steered her out. I said you were casing a job. Fair's fair. You cover for me with the boss, I smokescreen your night out.

LOU: Appreciated. That's thinking on your feet. I guess I misread you.

BARRY: Innocent mistake. You *should* be concerned about Shirley. A beautiful girl.

LOU: *(With calculation)* As is Lori. Especially naked.

(BARRY *leaps at* LOU *who goes for his gun in his shoulder holster. But of course, he comes up short. By the time he recovers and moves towards the gun on the table,* BARRY's *got the bead on him with his own piece.*

BARRY: I oughtta chill you right now.

LOU: *(Genuinely scared)* For what? For supporting your sister?

BARRY: Supporting??? How do you mean "supporting"? What do you two—

LOU: At the box office...by my patronage. She's a public entertainer... much admired I might add. An exotic dancer.

BARRY: *(Contemptuously)* A stripper.

LOU: Comes with the territory. Nothing happens. They've got bouncers. You should come with me sometime.

BARRY: Freak me out, why don'tcha??? Have you...no morals? I don't know what kind of family raised you, but—

LOU: Bettter than yours.

BARRY: Big deal. I can't go...and watch...my own sister...*disrobe.*

LOU: She's beautiful.

BARRY: Not to her brother. Clothed she's a knockout. *(Softening)* Ah...alright, Lou. You don't have siblings. You don't know about this brother-sister bond.

LOU: Evidently not.

BARRY: Well, it's in...in...intense.

LOU: Evidently.

BARRY: How's her career?

LOU: Fine. She's thinking of getting a boob job.

BARRY: *(Alarmed)* What's wrong with her boobs?

LOU: A reduction.

BARRY: *(Painfully)* Oh, no!

LOU: Except she's heard they irritate the areolas. I don't think she needs it. From a fully-clothed perspective, what do you think?

BARRY: I don't. And her...*boobs* are not her career.

LOU: Oh...theater.

(He pulls out a paperback version of Pinter's The Caretaker *and* The Dumb Waiter.*)*

LOU: She gave me this to read. No role for her but she says it's about us.

BARRY: *(Checking the book)* Gimmee a break.

LOU: You know it?

BARRY: *(Reciting from memory)* "Pinter, Harold. Drama, twentieth century, British. Call number 822.914 P-I-N."

LOU: You're amazing, Barr. Every librarian should be so astute. So you've read him.

BARRY: No, I'm not a reader. You know that.

LOU: Yeah, I could never figure how you got to be a librarian if you don't like to read.

BARRY: I like to catalogue. However, I do attend plays. Which is the real intent of theatre.

LOU: You've been Lori's inspiration.

BARRY: Lori, *the actress*, I trust.

LOU: Of course. Do you go to her stage performances?

BARRY: She hasn't had any stage performances.

LOU: On the contrary. She's a natural performer.

BARRY: *(Disdainfully)* Harold Pinter. Gimmee a break. *(Playing two British characters in conversation)* "I do." "But I don't." ...Pause. "I will." "But I won't." Pregnant pause. "I shall." "But I shant." Eight month pregnant pause. Harold Pinter. Wake me when it's over.

LOU: *(Thumbing through the text)* I dunno. I'm curious if it's about us.

BARRY: About us? Exactly my point. Borrrrrrring. Big time. Pinter's a minimalist.

LOU: Doesn't mince words.

BARRY: He's got so little to say.

LOU: He won the Nobel prize.

BARRY: B-F-D! Nobel endowed a peace prize from his war profiteering. Helllllooo! There's a guy that Bush could love. Swedes are fucked up.

LOU: Lori tells me it's about two assassins waiting for an assignment.

BARRY: We're not assassins. That's political. I don't even vote. I think of us as surreptitious dispatchers.

LOU: *(Referring to the title)* And we don't have a dumbwaiter.

BARRY: I think the title's metaphorical.

LOU: "Dumb Waiter". Singular. Two words. So, one of us is a dumb waiter? That would be you, Barry. You lay around the apartment all day.

BARRY: Someone's gotta wait for the assignment.

LOU: I'm out...I'm active...I'm sociable.

BARRY: They keep getting these preposterous orders for food. From upstairs.

LOU: That's not us. Are these guys gay?

BARRY: They never say.

LOU: How long is this play?

BARRY: I dunno. An hour.

LOU: They're straight. I can't imagine two queens in a room for an hour who'd let you forget they're gay.

(The phone rings.)

BARRY: The assignment.

LOU: Shit! I need sleep.

BARRY: *(Answering)* Good morning. "Barry and Lou's Dispatching".

(He giggles. LOU doesn't. BARRY gets serious.)

BARRY: Oh, hiya Shirley. *(Beat)* Yeah, he's here.

(He extends the phone to wary LOU.*)*

LOU: *(Bitterly)* You mean she wants to talk to *me*? *(Pause, then...)*
Ask her what she wants.

BARRY: Shirley, can I ask you what you want?

(Beat. He again extends the phone.)

BARRY: She wants to know if you'll take care of the kids.

LOU: For the weekend?

BARRY: *(To the phone)* For the weekend? *(To* LOU*)* For good.

*(*LOU *goes postal and* BARRY *hangs up in panic.* LOU *goes for the gun and aims it
at his partner.)*

LOU: I'm gonna waste you.

BARRY: I dare you.

*(*LOU *pulls the trigger. Click. He is dumbfounded.* BARRY *draws his own gun.)*

BARRY: How could you, Lou?

LOU: *(Scared)* G-G-Gee, Barr, I aimed over your head. You know I'd n-n-ever
shoot anyone face-to-face. I'd never try to off my ole buddy.

*(*BARRY *displays the bullets [or ammo clip].)*

LOU: YOU WOULD'VE SENT ME ON A JOB WITH NO AMMO? YOU'RE
MERCILESS!!!

BARRY: No, Lou. I'm efficient. However, I've just found a reason to live.

(The phone rings. LOU *picks it up in a rage.)*

LOU: You two-timing whore.

BARRY: Hey, watch how you talk to Shirley.

LOU: *(Sobering)* Uh, sorry Boss... A change of plans? No problem. I'm
adaptable.... Huh?... I meant "we're" adaptable. Barry and I. A slip of the
tongue... Brooklyn. No problem. Hit City. We know the turf... You want
whaaaat???... That's really gonna cost, Boss. Big time! You want us to cut
off this guy's genitalia?... "Genitalia"... That's just another name for them.

(Aside to surprised BARRY*)*

LOU: A little education is a detriment, here. *(Into the phone, wide-eyed)*
You mean, while he's alive? Boss, I got nothing against creative killing,
but— ...Boss, it could be a routine thing *after* he's dead. A little amateur
surgery. But— ...THEN STUFF 'EM IN HIS MOUTH?... THEN CUT HIS
HEAD OFF???

*(*BARRY *is appalled. He runs off and is heard puking mightily.)*

LOU: Boss, is this ever gonna cost... Then put his head in his home mailbox. What if they've got a slot? Y'know, for the mail?... You're sure? ...Gimmee the address. This isn't fair to the mailman.

(He gestures for returning BARRY *to write but he refuses.* LOU *jots.)*

LOU: Boss, this guy evidently rattled your cage. *(Shocked again)* He knocked up Natasha?

BARRY: The guy should be awarded. Valor above and beyond—

LOU: *(Into the phone)* Hey, Vladimer should be doing this. He should avenge his sister.... He wants the guy to marry her?

BARRY: Killing this guy would be an act of mercy.

LOU: *(Enthusiastically)* Sure I know a marriageable guy, Boss. Barry!

BARRY: *(Suspiciously)* No you don't, Lou.

LOU: He's looking for a girl. The boy is lovesick.

BARRY: Natasha? In your dreams.

LOU: *(Into the phone)* He tells me he dreams about Natasha.

BARRY: *(Grabbing the phone)* Unfortunately Boss, I've got herpes...HERPES... It's like V D. No, it won't kill her.... It may not matter to Natasha but it matters to me. Here, Lou. He wants you.

LOU: Hello? ...O K, good as done. We'll settle up later. But believe me, it won't be cheap. So long. *(Hanging up)* C'mon, buddy. We gotta job.

BARRY: Who?

LOU: Who knows? Who cares?

BARRY: Lou, I reiterate. I'm through. I don't feel it any more.

(He pushes the bullets towards LOU.*)*

BARRY: I've been to the edge myself, see. And I've made it back. So I appreciate the value of life.

LOU: Bullshit! Life is dirt cheap. And this is a difficult hit. Exceedingly so. I need help.

BARRY: So cheat a little.

LOU: On the boss? Are you nuts?

BARRY: Kill the guy first. Then cut off his *cojones*...stuff 'em in his mouth and then slice off his dome. Who's to know? It's not difficult. Just...well, yucky.

LOU: But usually their jaws clench shut when they die. You know that.

(They both reflect on this dilemma. Then...)

LOU: Can I borrow a shirt. This is going to get bloody.

BARRY: Which one?

LOU: Of yours? They're all expendable. (*He goes to a closet and dons a truly tacky shirt.*)

BARRY: Take a pair of pliers. To pry open his mouth.

LOU: Pliers won't open his mouth. They're like, for... (*Miming*) ...y' know, extracting, not expanding.

BARRY: How do I know? I'm not a mechanic. I'm an artist.

LOU: What???

BARRY: Well...I'm...uh, on the artsy track.

LOU: I've got it. A crowbar!

BARRY: You got it! It's in the Volvo.

LOU: (*Heading off*) You're not coming, huh? O K, then. There's no split. I keep the whole fee.

BARRY: As it should be.

LOU: (*Bitterly*) You...chickenshit bastard!

(LOU *exits with a slam.* BARRY *dials the phone.*)

BARRY: Shirley? ...It's me, baby. Listen, your husband just went out on a job. I'm comin' over, O K? God, I miss you.

(*Blackout*)

Scene Three

(*The same. Nighttime*)

(BARRY *stares out the window. He appears to be focused on an apartment across the way and a couple of floors higher.*)

(LOU *rushes in. He heads directly off and returns in a moment with a suitcase and some clothes.*)

BARRY: Hey, what's up?

LOU: I let him off the hook.

BARRY: What??? You never let *anyone* off the hook. You slaughter with ruthless efficiency. It's horrifying...albeit fascinating. Deadly calculation is your trademark...your signature.

LOU: You were my mentor, pal. Before your breakdown. By the way, I suggest that you pack, too.

BARRY: *(Pointing to the suitcases)* I'm packed.

(LOU stops, looks at BARRY. Then he runs to a dresser/cabinet and extracts more clothing.)

LOU: So, you we're leaving? I'd be holding the bag?

BARRY: That's not what I intended.

LOU: I blew the gig. You're off hook.

BARRY: The Ruskies don't know that I retired.

LOU: If you had been my partner, tonight—

BARRY: The guy would be toast, now?

LOU: You bet.

BARRY: No way. I've lost the killer instinct.

LOU: Well, your instinct to scram is intact. We're the targets, now.

BARRY: We've always been targeted.

LOU: We have? By whom?

BARRY: The cops.

LOU: Oh yeah, I nearly forgot. *(He smiles then starts laughing)* Don't make me laugh. The cops are looking for us in Little Italy. Or Harlem. I never worry about the cops. *(Sobering)* But the boss has dispatched shooters as we speak.

BARRY: That explains it then. *(Pointing out the window)* That empty apartment across the alley...

LOU: Yeah.

BARRY: It's no longer empty.

LOU: *(Cautiously looking out)* How can you tell if the lights are out?

BARRY: They brought no luggage...no furniture. Just a carrying case.

LOU: That'd be the gun.

BARRY: And a cylidrical bag.

LOU: Tripod. Well, they've gone out.

BARRY: Or maybe they're sitting in the dark...watching us.

(They both withdraw from the line of fire.)

LOU: What do these guys look like?

BARRY: They're girls. Very pretty.

LOU: *(Relieved)* Whewwwww. You had me worried there for a minute.

BARRY: Very unlikely shooters, huh? *Like us!*

LOU: *(Becoming cautious)* Well, y'know...at the shooting range—

BARRY: Wall-to-wall women.

LOU: If a guy wants to get laid in America, the shooting range is the perfect place.

BARRY: As long as he's not in the line of fire.

LOU: No, I don't mean *at* the range.

BARRY: And as long as he's not aggressive with the babe.

LOU: All types there...soccer moms...teachers...flight attendants...

BARRY: Guns are an occupational necessity for flight attend—

LOU: Teachers, too.

BARRY: So why did you spare this dude?

LOU: I got...sensitive.

BARRY: G'wan! That's absurd.

LOU: And inquisitive. I had to meet the guy who knocked up Natasha.

BARRY: Loser, huh?

LOU: No, believe it or not.

BARRY: But Natasha's a pig.

LOU: Not to this guy.

BARRY: How many senses is he missing?

LOU: Barry, they're in love.

BARRY: That's not like you, Lou. You don't have a romantic bone in your—

LOU: The guy was scared shitless. He knew I was there to ice him. But when he looked at me with tears in his eyes... *(He chokes up.)*

BARRY: You didn't deliver your trade mark shot-to-the-back-of-the-head?

LOU: Nah. I knew he was clean...unarmed. A college boy. I knew he wouldn't retaliate. I'm not brave but I'm instinctive.

BARRY: So what did the dude say?

LOU: "Tell Natasha I love her."

(The two reflect silently.)

BARRY: And you know something? I'll bet Natasha loves him.

LOU: Certainly Natasha loves him. If it winked at her, Natasha would love a stone. "Kid", I asked him, "What am I missing here? What's Natasha got?" He says that she's hotter than a nymphomaniac on speedballs.

BARRY: Natasha??? Whataya know. Who knew what was churning under that *babushka*?

LOU: But The Boss won't accept him. He's not Russian.

BARRY: Given the few Russians I know, that's a plus.

LOU: He's an American.

BARRY: *(Miffed)* Well, too fuckin' bad. I knew The Boss was a hypocrite. Making hay in the land of the free. AND avoiding taxes.

LOU: So, at the moment of truth, I faltered.

BARRY: But a greater truth may have emerged.

LOU: You got it, buddy! I reflected on my decadent past. I corrupted some people's lives.

BARRY: And you *ended* other people's lives. *(He giggles.)*

LOU: Not funny, Barry. My wife rejects me. My best friend rejects me.

BARRY: Who's that?

LOU: You!

BARRY: *(Surprised)* Me???

LOU: See what I mean? Aren't I *your* best friend?

BARRY: *(Ponders)* Well, you would be if I had any friends.

LOU: What about Shirley?

BARRY: She's more than a friend.

(LOU goes mute then starts to cry. BARRY consoles him.)

BARRY: Hey Lou, ease up. There's nothing between Shirley and me.

LOU: Nothing?

BARRY: Nothing.

LOU: Then you'll stop seeing her?

BARRY: For what? If there was something' between us I'd see your point. But since there's nothing there then why bother? We'd just be catering to your whim. You've got to outgrow that dependency.

LOU: My wife rejects me for my best friend. Though he doesn't even consider me a friend.

BARRY: Lou, if I thought you were a friend I never would've gotten close to Shirley.

LOU: I thought there was nothing between you two.

BARRY: It's relative.

LOU: What the fuck does that— ...Did you sleep with her???

BARRY: Don't misconstrue. Nothing happens when you sleep.

LOU: Don't give me your semantic bullshit.

BARRY: Lou, Shirley's coming apart at the seams. You know that. She said that much more time with you and she'd do something extreme. I didn't want her hurting the kids.

LOU: Wow, she's that far gone?

BARRY: I feared for your kids, Lou.

LOU: You're a decent guy, Barr. *(Wiping his eyes)* Well, it struck me last night. I'd be the one getting hit one of these days.

BARRY: That's not like you, Lou. The consummate professional. But you're right. We're next. Just like in that play. *(Pointing to the paperback on the table)*

LOU: Oh right, the menacing Mister Pinter. Like he's really been down the criminal path.

BARRY: At the end of the play one of the hitmen bursts into the room occupied by the other.

LOU: Yeah...so? I just did that. That's not theatre. That's real life.

BARRY: The other guy's got the bead on him.

LOU: And he fires?

BARRY: *(Shaking his head)* It's all over.

LOU: You bet. For the poor jerk who invaded the room.

BARRY: No, the play ends before anything happens.

LOU: No gunshot?

BARRY: No gunshot!

LOU: I'd call that inconclusive.

BARRY: I'd call that Pinter.

LOU: Let me get this straight—

BARRY: It's a metaphor.

LOU: For what?

BARRY: For life.

LOU: Life's inconclusive?

BARRY: Of course.

LOU: We've concluded *lots* of lives.

BARRY: On *one* level.

LOU: The ultimate level.
So the lights dim on this play with this one schmuck confronting the shooter.

BARRY: —Who doesn't shoot.

LOU: That doesn't make sense. Shooters shoot.

BARRY: Oh, like theater has to make sense?

LOU: *(Gesturing the descending curtain)* The curtain comes down?

BARRY: Of sorts. *(Gesturing the lowering lights)* The lights come down.

LOU: *(Gesturing the ascending lights)* I thought that the lights come *up.*

BARRY: *(Gesturing the rising house lights)* The *house* lights come up.

LOU: Oh. *(Gesturing the lowering stage lights)* So the *stage* lights come down?

BARRY: Right. In lieu of a curtain.

LOU: If there had been a curtain, *(Gesturing the lowering curtain)* it would've come down?

BARRY: *(Gesturing closing curtains)* Unless it closed.

LOU: *(Gesturing closing then lowering curtains)* If the curtain had *not* closed...or come down—

BARRY: That's another play.

LOU: WELL, BETTER *THAT* PLAY SO WE KNOW WHO WINS!!!

BARRY: That's the point in this play. Nobody wins.

LOU: *(Angrily)* Certainly not the audience!

BARRY: There's no resolution. Like the lives we've been leading.

LOU: Wrong. Pinter wins. Big-time. He gets royalties for a play he couldn't finish. WHO MADE THIS GUY GOD???

BARRY: *(Gestures the descending dumbwaiter)* God is sending down the food orders in the dumbwaiter.

LOU: *(Pointing upwards)* We've got a transvestite junkie upstairs. Does that make him God?

BARRY: God can be whomever he wants to be. It's his ballgame.

LOU: If you've never read the play, how come you remember the details?

BARRY: I've *seen* the play. I remember call numbers without having read the books.

LOU: You're a regular idiot savant, Barry. But we've got a couple of goons bearing down on us.

BARRY: Goon*ettes.*

LOU: I'm outta here. It's been great, man. But you're no longer trustworthy. You'd rat me out to save your own ass.

BARRY: You *wouldn't?*

LOU: *(Shrugs)* This is *not* an ethical profession.

BARRY: I'm coming, too.

LOU: In your dreams, dude. You're too fixated on your sister.

BARRY: You're taking her with you?

LOU: Damn right.

BARRY: Well, that should work out fine.

LOU: How do you figure?

BARRY: I'm taking your wife.

(LOU chases BARRY around the room until BARRY produces a gun from the dresser. LOU retaliates with a gun from under a chair or a drawer. They wrestle around awkwardly until LOU gets the bead on BARRY who whines...)

BARRY: Mommyyyyy!

(BARRY then sucks his thumb. LOU aims at his head.)

LOU: Your Mommy can't help you now!

BARRY: GIVE IT UP, LOU! SHE LOVES ME. YOU CAN'T LOVE TWO WOMEN! ARE YOU STRINGIN' MY SISTER???

LOU: I'M IN LOVE WITH YOUR SISTER! AND SHE LOVES ME!

(They stop...reflect...)

LOU: What are we fighting about? I love your sister, not my wife.

BARRY: Well, she doesn't love you.

LOU: Who doesn't?

BARRY: Your wife.

LOU: Since when?

BARRY: Since ever.

LOU: She never loved me?

BARRY: Nope.

LOU: Good. No one gets hurt, then. I never loved her either.

BARRY: Geez, you two were living a lie for...fourteen years.

LOU: Was it that long?

(BARRY *nods.*)

LOU: We must've lied for sex. Love is based on truth, sex is based on lies.

BARRY: You might've loved each other if you ever told the truth.

LOU: True. But it might've ruined the sex. The things we did together...people who love don't do.

BARRY: Maybe we should keep the girls apart. Four people in my sister's country cottage...it could get fairly claustrophobic. We'll be upstate but we should stay homebound until the heat is off.

LOU: Six people. Plus kids.

BARRY: Six people??? Hey, it's not some boarding house that—

LOU: Natasha and her guy.

BARRY: Are you crazy?

LOU: I've never been so sane. The girl's a buffer.

BARRY: She could rat us out.

LOU: To whom? Her father? She hates him. She loves her guy. She'd kill anyone gunning for him. And even if the boss tracked her down there'd be no shoot-out. And Natasha assured me that no one will recognize her after the baby. She's gonna lose a hundred and fifty pounds. She's getting her stomach stapled.

(BARRY *winces.*)

LOU: She's throwing away all her peasant clothes. She's bathing...shaving her back....

BARRY: What some folks won't do for love.

LOU: She's getting new teeth.

BARRY: Good idea. Her teeth are her defining characteristic.

LOU: Her *lack* of teeth.

BARRY: Well, yeah.

(*A car horn sounds.* LOU *has crossed to the window and looks down.*)

LOU: Lori's driving the Volvo.

BARRY: *(Alarmed)* HEY, GET AWAY FROM THE WINDOW!!!

LOU: *(Darting from the shooter's range)* Whewwww! Gotta be careful. Thanks, buddy. We're not out of the woods, yet.

BARRY: Never will be.

LOU: Yeah. *(Reflects)* Maybe we shouldn't subject the girls to this...pressure.

BARRY: It's a trade off. They get love in return.

LOU: Not exactly. We get love, they get love. But what's the trade off for putting their lives in jepordy?

BARRY: *(Ponders)* Fidelity.

LOU: *(Staring, then lightly...)* Fidelity? If Natasha rounded into shape, you'd bump off her boyfriend.

BARRY: I wouldn't screw her with *your* dick. If you're going straight Lou, then so am I.

LOU: I'm going straight.

BARRY: Shirley said she didn't want me to wind up like you.

LOU: The nerve of her.

BARRY: I defended you...said you were a good guy...the killings aside.

(BARRY takes out his gun. LOU freezes. BARRY toys with the moment. Then he smiles and puts it down. LOU relaxes.)

BARRY: This should make it official. I'm leaving my gun behind. How about you?

LOU: I'm leaving my life behind. But not my gun.

(The car horn sounds, again.)

BARRY: What do we do now?

LOU: I've got some dough saved. Despite Shirley's extravagance. And Lori makes good money. We can lay low for awhile. I'll tend to your sister's garden. You?

BARRY: Lori said she'd try and get Shirley some work stripping.

LOU: I thought you objected to that line of work.

BARRY: It's different with Shirley. She's not a blood relative.

LOU: I should hope not.

BARRY: She has low self-esteem after those years with you. This is therapeutic.

LOU: So what will you do?

BARRY: I want to try acting after the heat is off.

LOU: From killing to acting isn't a moral redemption. But the Ruskies will never find you.

BARRY: You think I'd never be cast?

LOU: I think they'd never see a play.

(The car horn sounds two-three times.)

LOU: I should warn you, Barr. Shirley has a ferocious temper. And an affinity for butcher knives.
C'mon, if you're coming.

(LOU *exits.* BARRY *stares blankly, then looks at the gun, then picks it up and returns it to his shoulder holster. As the lights are fading...)*

BARRY: *(To himself)* An old habit dies hard. Especially when you're good at it. *(Shouting)* Hey Buddy, wait for me.

(Grabbing his suitcase, he heads off as the lights come down.)

END OF PLAY

BAD GIRLS

CHARACTERS & SETTING

MOLLY, *late thirties*
ARLENE, *late thirties.*

Time: the present

Place: A vacant apartment with a window. A table and two chairs. Brighton Beach, Brooklyn, NY

Suggested music: Bad Girls *by Bill (Smokey) Robinson and The Miracles, circa 1960 or* Bad Girls *by Donna Summer, 1979. There are other songs with the same title.*

Scene One

(The room is bare save a couple of chairs up-side-down atop a kitchen table. The women at the open door wear dark sunglasses. They have two leather [?] carrying cases containing a high-powered rifle [with scope] and a tripod. They'll enter, upright the chairs and begin to assemble both [ARLENE, the rifle and MOLLY, the tripod]. ARLENE also has a laptop in a case which she sets aside.)

(The women are well-groomed, well-dressed but informal. They could be successful career women. Or soccer moms. They are not typical mob babes though they are setting up for a kill. The sunglasses come off.)

(MOLLY peers out the window and slightly downward at an adjacent apartment as ARLENE starts to assemble the gun. MOLLY is new to this and fascinated. ARLENE is the veteran, all business.)

ARLENE: Well?

MOLLY: Not a sign.

ARLENE: Doesn't look good.

MOLLY: It does to me. Maybe we can go home now.

ARLENE: You are laboring under a misapprehension, Molly. If those boys went missing we can't just pack up and go home. Then *we* could have to go missing.

MOLLY: I don't understand this. These guys haven't done anything wrong.

ARLENE: They failed to do a hit, that's wrong. So we've been hired to do a hit *on them*. If we walk off the job then a pair will be hired to smoke *us*.

MOLLY: And if we dodge the shooters sent to kill us...

ARLENE: A pair would be dispatched to kill *them*.

MOLLY: This could go on...

ARLENE: Interminably. Like, for infinity. Y' know, worst case scenario.

MOLLY: Not for *us*. And for society. No more killing. *(Smiles)*

ARLENE: An ideal world. And all because the first marks—

MOLLY: —"went missing".

ARLENE: Exactly.

MOLLY: I never heard that phrase before.

ARLENE: "An ideal world"? You must have.

MOLLY: "Went missing". It's like...British, I guess.

ARLENE: I'm not British.

MOLLY: Course not. You're from Long Island. Like me. Do you ever visit?

ARLENE: Long Island? Of course.

MOLLY: Britain.

ARLENE: Well, ...yeah. Once. For a week.

MOLLY: Can't be osmosis, Arlene. For one week in Britain you're a bit pretentious.

ARLENE: *(Staring at* MOLLY, *then...)* Molly, can we focus on the job?

MOLLY: Hardly my idea of a job.

ARLENE: Tell me about it. No Social Security. No retirement—

MOLLY: Lots of folks in this line don't live to retire.

ARLENE: *(A critical look, then...)* No unemployment compensation. No hospitalization. Medical care is important.

MOLLY: Burial insurance.

ARLENE: Hey, enough of that!

MOLLY: You can never have enough burial insurance in this job.

ARLENE: Cancel that mind-set. To get ahead in this game you must see the glass as half-full, not half-empty.

MOLLY: I don't even *have* a glass.

ARLENE: No benefits on this job but the pay is great.

MOLLY: MURDER IS NOT MY IDEA OF A JOB!!!

ARLENE: Parrrrrrrdon me!!! Will you turn back the do-re-mi???

MOLLY: Of course not. Money's the solitary factor.

ARLENE: Not for me.

MOLLY: Not for you? Is this an aesthetic high? Murder as art form?

ARLENE: It's a social corrective.

MOLLY: Lemmee get this straight. You see the killing of two men as a... —don't let me misquote you—as a "social corrective"?

ARLENE: Well, y' know...in context.

MOLLY: I guess you'd really get off on nuclear warfare.

ARLENE: *(Suspiciously)* Are you having second thoughts?

MOLLY: About shooting people? Oh, *I* don't object *personally.*
It's my conscience that keeps getting in the way.

ARLENE: You've weighed the pros and cons...

MOLLY: *(Nods)* The cons have it.

ARLENE: From my P O V, it's win-win.

MOLLY: Naturally. For you it could be a police commendation...
a pay raise, probably.

ARLENE: This is hardly police work.

MOLLY: Could be. You're paid to get rid of bad guys. But me, I'm a
vigilante. It's the gallows. *(She mimes herself hanging, her hand on an
imaginary noose, eyes bulging, tongue extended, legs twitching as she gags.)*

ARLENE: Or a payday.

MOLLY: *If* he pays.

ARLENE: Why would he not pay? As a cop, I've got The Boss by the short
hairs. *(Beat)* And there's no more gallows.

MOLLY: The electric chair.

ARLENE: There's no capital punishment in this state.

MOLLY: For me, they'd reinstate.
Yeah, you've got The Boss by the gonads. But I'm not a cop.

ARLENE: So what? I'll cover for you. I'm your alibi.

MOLLY: You don't have much credibility as a cop. Y'know, moonlighting as
an assassin.

ARLENE: Nobody knows. Except you and The Boss. And I see it as
experience...training.

MOLLY: At what? Breaking your promise to uphold the law?

ARLENE: Experience at shooting bad guys. Remember, we stipulated..
."Bad guys only".

MOLLY: How do we know we aren't shooting law-abiding citizens?

ARLENE: The Boss doesn't deal with law-abiding citizens. Why would he
shoot good guys?

MOLLY: True. I imagine *you* don't care if bad guys get it.

ARLENE: True. One could argue that this is extra-curricular.

MOLLY: *One* could argue that. You'd be the one...and *only* one.

ARLENE: My experience is hard-earned.

MOLLY: *(Reacting to this)* Arlene, everyone sympathizes with you... what you went through. But two wrongs don't make—

ARLENE: *(Interrupting)* I still think it's amazing. You and me. Partners.

MOLLY: We should be a good team. Y'know, since we go all the way back to high school.

ARLENE: Cheerleaders together...student council.

MOLLY: Prom committee.

ARLENE: I wasn't on the prom committee.

MOLLY: You weren't? I could've sworn that —

ARLENE: That was my sister.

MOLLY: It was?

ARLENE: My twin.

MOLLY: Oh...yeah. Yeah, ...Monique. I'd get you two mixed—

ARLENE: *(Testily)* We were entirely different.

MOLLY: You looked the same.

ARLENE: I was high honors. She dropped out of school.

MOLLY: You were the big shot in student council.

ARLENE: Long time ago. Things change.

MOLLY: You hardly ever noticed me.

ARLENE: I noticed you. You were head cheerleader.

MOLLY: Not an enduring sort of honor. Y'know, a fleeting thing.

ARLENE: You got all the guys.

MOLLY: I got the jocks. Well...not all of them.

ARLENE: That was Merilee Gardner.

MOLLY: Uh-uh, they all got *her.*

(ARLENE *mimes a shot to her temple with her finger.*)

ARLENE: Merilee killed herself, y' know.

MOLLY: Oh, wow! Why?

ARLENE: She didn't wanna live. Too many guys I guess.

MOLLY: That's no reason to kill yourself.

ARLENE: All it takes is one.

MOLLY: Bullet?

ARLENE: Guy.

MOLLY: I *usually* got the ones I wanted.

ARLENE: Like flies on shit...you should pardon the analogy.

MOLLY: *(Peeved)* You still have that chip on your shoulder from high school.

ARLENE: *(Shrugs)* Entitled. My father was in jail.

MOLLY: Big deal. I knew that.

ARLENE: You knew???

MOLLY: Everyone knew.

ARLENE: *Everyone* knew?

MOLLY: Sing Sing.

ARLENE: Why didn't you tell me?

MOLLY: You didn't *know*?

ARLENE: Certainly, I knew!!! He was my father, fer Chrissakes. Why didn't you tell me you knew?

MOLLY: I don't know. I didn't know you that well.

ARLENE: You didn't know me that well but you knew me well enough to know that my father was in jail.

MOLLY: What would've been the point?

ARLENE: I could have faced the truth.

MOLLY: You say you *knew* the truth.

ARLENE: Yeah, but I denied it.

MOLLY: If you denied the truth—

ARLENE: I just said I did!

MOLLY: So, you lied.

ARLENE: True, I lied.

MOLLY: But you wouldn't have lied if we had told the truth.

ARLENE: "We"?

MOLLY: Your classmates.

ARLENE: Uh...yeah. I guess.

MOLLY: So you're blaming us for—

ARLENE: Uh, I...dunno. Where is this going?

MOLLY: It's going nowhere, Arlene since you're blaming your long-ago classmates for your lies.

ARLENE: I didn't say that.

MOLLY: For your fucked-up life.

ARLENE: I'm not complaining.

MOLLY: Why not blame your father?

ARLENE: Because my father never lied to me.

MOLLY: Naturally. He was away. In jail. What was he in for?

ARLENE: You tell me, Nancy Drew.

MOLLY: *(After a quizzical stare)* I'm trying to help you through this, Arlene.

ARLENE: Arson. He set fire to our house.

MOLLY: Wow, how much time did he get?

ARLENE: Thirty years.

MOLLY: Wow, thirty years. That's heavy.

ARLENE: We were inside. Listen, I'd rather not talk about my father.

MOLLY: Me neither. What a scuzz. Arlene, maybe we should settle something before we go any further.

ARLENE: I think I know what's coming.

(Somewhat evasively, MOLLY goes to the window and peers across at the targeted apartment.)

ARLENE: Anything?

MOLLY: *(Returning)* Nothing.

ARLENE: So...?

MOLLY: Anthony D'Arcangelo.

ARLENE: Oh, man...pick, pick, pick away at an old scab, why dontcha?

MOLLY: You didn't think he was an old scab at the time.

ARLENE: Not at the time. But have you seen him lately?

MOLLY: An old scab...our Tony D'Arc?

ARLENE: Sabotage our relationship, why don'tcha?

MOLLY: You and Tony? Still?

ARLENE: You and ME! *Our* relationship. We have a prospering partnership, here. A lucrative sideline. But you have to go and resurrect our one, serious, long-ago conflict. Ancient history. What is it we have to "settle"?

MOLLY: The Tony D'Arc...abduction. For lack of a better word.

ARLENE: "Better words" don't apply to Tony. Only worse words. Believe me, Molly. I did you a favor. And I didn't *steal* him.

MOLLY: Precisely, Arlene. I gave him up.

ARLENE: Well, I'll take issue with that.

MOLLY: Later, *you* gave him up.

ARLENE: Uh...I dunno about that, either.

MOLLY: O K, "relinquished", then. You relinquished him to—

ARLENE: That Asian chick. She stole him, actually.

MOLLY: Becky Woo.

ARLENE: Now, she *did* give him up.

MOLLY: He hit a wall with her.

ARLENE: Head-on.

MOLLY: She knew what he was up to. Smart people those Asians.

ARLENE: Maybe they're just less promiscuous.

MOLLY: *(Critically) Promiscuous?*

ARLENE: Uh... vulnerable. Vulnerable to... Tony's seductiveness.

MOLLY: Because I was *not* promiscuous.

ARLENE: I didn't mean you.

MOLLY: ...despite what the guys said.

ARLENE: They said it about lots of us.
Notice Tony never moved on an Italian girl.

MOLLY: You bet. But he married one.

ARLENE: I wasn't surprised. Were you surprised?

MOLLY: Nothing about Tony surprised me. Speaking for myself understand, Tony and I had more than a...well, we had a serious relationship. Heavy. More than kid's stuff. Can you say that, Arlene?

ARLENE: *(Mulls this over, then...)* I can. Did he tell you he was serious?

MOLLY: In just so many words.

ARLENE: More than three? Because that's all he needed with me.

MOLLY: He said, *(Mimicking Tony)* "You're...the one". There. Three words.

ARLENE: *(Surprised)* He said... *(Pointing to herself and mimicking Tony)* ...*I* was the one?

MOLLY: No, no, *I* was the one! Why would he tell me *you* were the one.

ARLENE: Yeah, right. Especially when he was gettin' into your pants.

MOLLY: *(Pause...stare, then...)* Tony wasn't stupid.

ARLENE: He certainly wasn't smart.

MOLLY: True. But he could be clever. Especially if there was nookie at stake.

ARLENE: Manipulative...when it came to sex.

MOLLY: Just a pissant little John Travolta. Remember *Saturday Night Fever?*

ARLENE: *(Quizzically)* I never saw it.

MOLLY: Everybody saw it.

ARLENE: I was too poor.

MOLLY: For a movie?

ARLENE: Destitute.

MOLLY: What about your dates?

ARLENE: My *dates* were too poor.

MOLLY: For a movie? Maybe they just told you that so you'd *give* it away.

ARLENE: *(Threartening)* Hey Molly, I could rip your—

MOLLY: Relax! Only kiddin'.

ARLENE: *(Beat...settling down)* I was ashamed. Monique and I had to share clothes. That's why Monique dropped out. We ran out of clothes.

MOLLY: That was a shame.

ARLENE: So be it.

MOLLY: It was a good flick...*Saturday Night Fever.*

ARLENE: *(After a take to* MOLLY*)* It was irrelevant.

MOLLY: You didn't see it. How do you know it's irrelevant?

ARLENE: A bunch of kids from Brooklyn who spend their lives dancing? That's relevance? .

MOLLY: It's a movie. Movies aren't supposed to be relevant.

ARLENE: Then what's the point?

MOLLY: The point is to just relax...chill out for a couple of hours watching Tony and his chicks. *(She breaks into the film's disco dance.)*

ARLENE: Tony?

MOLLY: Tony Manero.

ARLENE: In the movie?

MOLLY: Sure. Our Tony was imitating the movie Tony.

ARLENE: I wish I'd seen the movie.

MOLLY: Rent it.

ARLENE: Too late, now.

MOLLY: It's in the video store.

ARLENE: It's too late *now* to relate to *then*.

MOLLY: Rent it anyway. For the dancing. *(She breaks into the couple's "spin" dance in the film.)*

ARLENE: *(Shakes her head)* If I wanted to see dancing, I'd rent *Swan Lake*.

MOLLY: *(Stops, then quizzically)* Swan Lake? Who's in it?

ARLENE: Nobody. It's ballet.

MOLLY: *(Doing a disdainful mock-pirouette)* Ballet? Put me to sleep. You were always the artsy one.

ARLENE: Culture's not a shameful thing, Molly. Maybe you'd be in a better place now if you nurtured your artistry. *(She has finished assembling the rifle.)*

MOLLY: Wow, you know your way around that thing.

ARLENE: An acquired aptitude.

MOLLY: *(To the window)* I don't see any movement. I'll finish the tripod and we'll set up.

ARLENE: No, no! Not in daylight. After dark.

MOLLY: Oh, yeah. I get the picture.

ARLENE: This is not on-the-job training. It's very dangerous.

MOLLY: Hey Arlene, if you were Miss Artsy-Fartsy then why'd you go out with a goombah like Tony D'Arc?

ARLENE: *(Shaking her head)* He was relevant. Not a movie. A living, breathing sensitive —

MOLLY: Sensitive??? I once asked him why he left me for you.

ARLENE: I did *not* steal him away, Molly.

MOLLY: Granted, Arlene. He told me, *(Mimicking Tony running his fingers through his hair)* "Arlene's gettin' straight As. T'inks she's better 'an de rest of us. But I'm gonna drag her back inta de dirt and she'll love it."

ARLENE: He said that? Verbatim?

MOLLY: *(Faking her awareness)* Absolutely. Or words to that effect.

ARLENE: Geez, here I thought I was elevating him.

MOLLY: You couldn't elevate Tony with a forklift.

ARLENE: Well, maybe I stooped to Tony's level. But I didn't love it.
And I didn't stay very long.

MOLLY: He met his match with Becky.

ARLENE: He called her his "Bamboo Bimbo" once too often. What a scumbag.

MOLLY: Hey, Arlene...about Tony...

ARLENE: *(Raising her right hand to slap* MOLLY's *palm)* Fuhgedaboudit!

MOLLY: *(Without reciprocation)* Forget about it?

ARLENE: Yeah, forget about Tony. A scumbag.

MOLLY: Easier said than done. *(Pointing outward)* Hey, what if Tony should
stroll into that room?

ARLENE: I'd do what I'm paid to do. I'd blow him away.

MOLLY: *(Apprehensively)* You mean you'd pull the trigger?

ARLENE: Of course that's what I mean. Whaddaya think?

MOLLY: Aim for his nuts. Then let me finish him off.

ARLENE: A shot to his nuts *would* finish him off. That's where his heart is.
Tony doesn't *stroll* any more. I went to our reunion this year. We knew
Tony two hundred pounds ago.

MOLLY: Wow, that's how many pounds a year?

ARLENE: He still clears the floor when he dances. But they don't watch him
anymore. They *dodge* him.

MOLLY: I knew I should've gone to the reunion.

ARLENE: *(Going for her purse or wallet)* I got his number. He slipped it to me
on the sly. Sorta like a coy rhinoceros. *(She produces Tony's card.)*

MOLLY: He still wanted to get it on?

ARLENE: *(Looking at the card)* I told him his tool was buried too deep in fat.
He manages a car wash in Hempstead. *(She extends the card.)*

MOLLY: What do I want with a car wash guy.

ARLENE: *(Mock-impressed)* Manager!

*(*MOLLY *takes it, tears it in half and tosses it.)*

ARLENE: Hey! Evidence. Pocket the card. You gotta start thinking like a cop.

MOLLY: Good thinking, officer.
Hey! That's it. We stuff these two guys and leave Tony's card.

ARLENE: "*Stuff* these guys"? What're you, a taxidermist?

MOLLY: *(Reflectively) Not that I know of.*

ARLENE: We *stiff* these guys—

MOLLY: —and leave Tony's card.

ARLENE: That'd be a hoot! But no, it's not in the game plan.

(MOLLY *pockets the two parts of the card.)*

MOLLY: I didn't have anyone to take to the reunion.

ARLENE: I thought you were married.

MOLLY: I couldn't have brought Bernie. We were at war, then.

ARLENE: Not shooting?

MOLLY: Pissing.

ARLENE: *(Shrugging)* Pissing's better.

MOLLY: Safer.

ARLENE: Except...y'know... Sometimes you hafta shoot. *(Gesturing towards the target)*

MOLLY: Now we're...estranged...apart.

ARLENE: You would've been right at home at the reunion. It was like a lonely hearts club. Kids?

MOLLY: He's got 'em. For now.
You?

ARLENE: We've split, my ole man and me. No kids. I don't see them as relevant.

MOLLY: Anyone I knew?

ARLENE: No one I knew. The reunion was a revelation. The people we knew were not the ones who were there... not anymore.

MOLLY: Like who?

ARLENE: Well...like Harry Grossman.

MOLLY: "Gross"?

ARLENE: The same. But not the same. He turned it around. We wrote him off but he's a big-time dentist.

MOLLY: What's his specialty?

ARLENE: *(After an incredulous look) Teeth*...what else?

MOLLY: I wouldn't care if he's a dental *surgeon*. I still wouldn't let those fingers in my mouth. Who knows where they've been?

ARLENE: Of course there was the flip side. The ones who peaked early.

MOLLY: Anthony D'Arcangelo.

ARLENE: A shadow of himself. A large shadow.

MOLLY: Maybe I'm his female counterpart. From head cheerleader to gun moll. *(She does a mini-routine miming her pom-pom days then segueing into "pistols" in each hand. Quietly...)* Rah-rah, bang-bang...rah-rah, bang-bang.

ARLENE: That's different. Cheerleaders *usually* peak in high school. *(A dig at* MOLLY*)* The top of their bell curve.

MOLLY: This gig isn't permanent. I'm sort of a temp assassin. I've still got a future...legitimate.

ARLENE: Of course you do. *We* do. And we're not gun molls. They're gang groupies. We're societal readjusters. Paid employees. Well-paid. And with my salary as a cop I make something commensurate to my student council colleagues.

MOLLY: *(Proudly)* Wow! Societal readjusters. But how many of those kids would have done this?

ARLENE: *Lots*! If they could. I was well-screened...tested, so to speak. We qualified, you and I. Psychologically.

MOLLY: I figured I was psychologically *mal*adjusted.

ARLENE: Maladjustment is an asset for this job.

MOLLY: Maybe I'm turning a sow's ear into a silk purse.

ARLENE: What's the sow's ear?

MOLLY: My life.

ARLENE: Quit your bellyachin'. You're to be commended. This is not a walk-on job.

MOLLY: Man, if anyone had told me years ago that we'd be partners—

ARLENE: You have trouble with that, Molly? Me as a partner?

MOLLY: No, not at all. You're so defensive. I just thought—

ARLENE: Cause if you do, you can split. I don't need a lukewarm partner. I never thought you were one of those spoiled rich kids back in school.

MOLLY: I don't mind being your partner. I just never thought we'd be partners in crime.

ARLENE: Something struck me when I saw you at the shooting range. You were so intense. And such a great shot.

MOLLY: When you're dedicated, it comes easy. *(She pantomimes her riflery as they talk. Taking dead aim down the fantasy barrel, she fakes about six rounds with intensity.)*

ARLENE: I noticed. At first I thought you were a bad shot. You never hit the target's heart. But you always hit the same spot.

MOLLY: I blasted many a groin.

ARLENE: And I said to myself, "Hey, I know that babe. Molly Murphy... from high school." You displayed a killer potential out there.

MOLLY: *(Tensely)* Men...men have...well...provoked me.

ARLENE: Yeah, men...the usual suspects. At first I thought about recommending you to the N Y P D. Y'know, as a sniper. But since The Boss encouraged me to look for a new partner—

MOLLY: What happened to your last partner?

ARLENE: Oh, she made a bundle and opened up a daycare. All my partners moved on. And up.

MOLLY: Did you get a commission?

ARLENE: For recruiting you? Well...yeah. A small one.

MOLLY: Found money. I was ready.

ARLENE: But you didn't know it. I had to psych you.

MOLLY: I was psyched. Men have ruined my life. Just like yours.

ARLENE: Well, not exactly.

MOLLY: What do you mean? Those guys that killed your mother... it was in all the papers. A random drive-by shooting.

ARLENE: It wasn't random. My father had ripped them off. But they weren't most men.

MOLLY: I can see why The Boss recruited you. Easy pickin's.

ARLENE: The Boss sent his son, Vladimer. A smooth operator. He scouted me. I was a rookie cop. I'd sit in the park every morning before duty. I had to compose myself or I'd kill someone on the job. Vladimer came by one day, asked to sit down. Said he'd seen me on T V. He called me... *(Russian accent)* ..."De cop d'ot justice denied."

MOLLY: "De cop d'ot justice denied." Cool.

ARLENE: He seemed sincere. Not like those T V assholes asking me how I felt.

MOLLY: What's to ask? Your mom was murdered and the killers walked... on a technicality.

ARLENE: Vladimer gave me this B S about how it wouldn't happen back in Russia. About how there were clandestine groups who administered... "d' proper punishment. An eye for an eye".

MOLLY: This job is easy for a cop. The law's on your side.

ARLENE: Every mark I take out has a big time record. I check. It's a prerequisite. No innocent bystanders. I make a civic contribution.

MOLLY: Also a contribution to your bank account. It doesn't bother you to work for the Russian underworld?

ARLENE: Hardly. They wiped out Mom's killers. *Gratis* It's not like spying. I'm not betraying my country. They want regular folks like you and me. *(Pointing outwardly)* And these two we're about to ice—

MOLLY: Poor guys.

ARLENE: Those "poor guys" are killers.

MOLLY: So are you.

ARLENE: And *you*! Or you will be when we croak these guys.

MOLLY: But maybe they're innocent. We're offing them without proof.

ARLENE: Think of them as Iraqis.

MOLLY: I guess Russians excell at this.

ARLENE: *(Nods)* Assassinations, yeah. The first thing The Boss asked about you, "Is she Italian?" He won't hire Italians. They're stereotypes. He's got a C P A hitman, a stock broker, a librarian, teachers—

MOLLY: Well, they're underpaid.

ARLENE: A coupla college athletes—

MOLLY: A logical source.

ARLENE: Lawyers.

MOLLY: Natural-born killers. My ex, for one.

ARLENE: A hundred or so years ago we could've done this on the frontier.

MOLLY: Not women.

ARLENE: Well, maybe not.

MOLLY: We owe this to the Womens' Movement..

ARLENE: God love those girls.

MOLLY: We've always been smarter than men. Now we're gettin' the muscle.

ARLENE: Give him credit. The Boss is progressive. Not like the Mafia.

MOLLY: Obsolete.

ARLENE: He's computerized his whole operation.

MOLLY: You don't think he's on the stock exchange, do you?

ARLENE: At the academy we were always told to zero in on "swarthy" types. But they never told us to consider women. The Boss is one step ahead of us.

MOLLY: "Us"?

ARLENE: The police.

MOLLY: These two guys we're gonna hit...they're sure not goombahs.

ARLENE: One went to Yale according to his internet profile. A Whiffenpoof, even.

(ARLENE *checks the target.*)

MOLLY: Anything?

ARLENE: Nothing.

MOLLY: They've split.

ARLENE: Then we're in trouble.

MOLLY: Oh God, my first assignment. I lasted longer at Walmart.

ARLENE: You worked for Walmart?

MOLLY: In the office. For a second. I got fired.

ARLENE: Lucky.

MOLLY: I guess so. But if you screwed up at Walmart they didn't shoot you. Listen, if these two guys have split why are we responsible? It's not our fault.

ARLENE: It's not personal.

MOLLY: That's assuring.

ARLENE: It's pragmatic. Sort of "shooter ethics". If we did the job, we'd never squeal. If we *didn't*, we might.

MOLLY: *(Nervously)* But I'm no squealer. I wasn't raised that way.

(ARLENE *just looks at her.*)

ARLENE: You weren't raised to kill people, either.
Relax. These boys are probably just out gettin' laid.

MOLLY: What makes you say that?

ARLENE: *(Indicating out the window)* Would you take a girl to an apartment like that for sex?

MOLLY: I wouldn't take a girl *anywhere* for sex!!!

ARLENE: I mean would a guy take—

MOLLY: It's enough that I shoot guys. Now I'm expected to sleep with girls?

ARLENE: Geez, given your experience with men, I figured you for—

MOLLY: My problems with men were never sexual, they were emo—
...emo— ...emo—

ARLENE: ENOUGH!!! I meant that no self-respecting guy would take a woman to a dump like that. *(Indicating the guys' apartment)*

MOLLY: They're not self-respecting. They're assassins.

ARLENE: Criminy!

MOLLY: *(Pause)* Tony would.

ARLENE: Would what?

MOLLY: Tony did. He took me to his brother's apartment.

ARLENE: Oh right. I nearly forgot.

MOLLY: *You*, too?

ARLENE: Not on your life. A pigsty. I turned around and walked out.

MOLLY: You did? That was admirable. That showed class...dignity.
It showed him that you weren't some cheap tramp...some slutty bimbo.

ARLENE: You walked out, too?

MOLLY: No, I stayed. *(Beat)* We got it on. But I should've split. He'd have respected me.

ARLENE: Bullshit! He didn't think any more of me. Let's face it. We got used.

MOLLY: I could kill the fucker. Especially now that I kill for money.
He ruined my life.

ARLENE: *(Staring at her)* How??? Are you serious? That was half-a-lifetime ago. I recovered from him like...well, like the twenty-four hour flu.

MOLLY: He wasn't the twenty-four hour flu with me. It may have been a dalliance with you. But...I don't dally.

ARLENE: Then you must...you must blame *me*.

MOLLY: *(Pause)* Not...not really, Arlene. I identify with you.

ARLENE: Get over it, kid. If you saw him at the reunion you'd have knelt down and thanked The Lord.

MOLLY: *(Smiles)* You think so.

ARLENE: And his wife looked *very* unhappy.

MOLLY: *(Ecstatically)* Really?

ARLENE: Very.

MOLLY: Swell!

ARLENE: You're better off. You gotta husband...two kids. Sort of.

(MOLLY doesn't respond. ARLENE notices then looks at her watch.)

ARLENE: Hey, gotta go. *(Starting off)*

MOLLY: *(Surprised)* Gotta go? Go where?

ARLENE: The Police Academy. I teach a class.

MOLLY: In law enforcement???

ARLENE: Whataya think, finger painting?

MOLLY: *(Pointing out the window)* What about...

ARLENE: Hold the fort.

MOLLY: You're taking time out from a murder to teach crime prevention???

ARLENE: Life's funny that way. So, stay focused. They'll return.

MOLLY: What do I do?

ARLENE: Shoot 'em.

MOLLY: *(Stunned)* By myself???

ARLENE: They'll never know.

MOLLY: Why do I need *you*, then?

ARLENE: You don't. I'm strictly backup.

MOLLY: Then back me up. I'm new at this.

ARLENE: Bull! I saw you on the shooting range. You're a pro.

MOLLY: With a gun, maybe. But not at killing.

ARLENE: You mastered the technique. Killing comes next. A natural outgrowth.

MOLLY: What're you, N R A?

ARLENE: Trust me. I was in the military, remember? You handled that gun with supreme confidence. In the service, those types were stone killers.

MOLLY: You were in the military?

ARLENE: Yeah, after college. Nobody wanted a Womens' Studies major.
I had to learn a trade.

MOLLY: You did *that.*

ARLENE: It was no stretch after Desert Storm. Just icing some more bad guys.

MOLLY: These guys we're lining up...they're not enemies.

ARLENE: They're potential. If they're hit men, they could target *us* some day.
This is all Darwinian.

MOLLY: You mean human advancement?

ARLENE: No! Survival of the fittest.

MOLLY: I keep wanting to think this over.

ARLENE: Too late. No thinking. No turning back.
I'm off.

MOLLY: *(Panicked)* Call in sick. I need help, here!

ARLENE: I can't. I need my sick days.

MOLLY: What for?

ARLENE: This! ...Moonlighting!

MOLLY: Somehow I think of moonlighting...well, as clerking at 7-11.

ARLENE: Is that what you want, clerking at—

MOLLY: No, no, then *I* might get shot.

ARLENE: So, quit your bitchin'! I have a bright future in the department.

MOLLY: You could administer torture.

ARLENE: Not funny. I intend to be the first woman commissioner. I'll be
back after class. Hold the fort. If you ice these guys, just pack up and go
home. We'll settle up later.

MOLLY: Gimmee your cellphone number.

ARLENE: Nothin' doin'. I'm unlisted. *(She exits immediately.)*

MOLLY: *(Befuddled, to herself)* She's unlisted??? It's not like I'm soliciting for
some charity.

*(It's evening and the room has darkened. MOLLY sets up the rifle with a telescopic
sight on the tripod so that she'll have a perfect shot. She lines up her sight then
relaxes since the opposite apartment is still darkened. She gets out her cellphone
and dials. Soon...)*

MOLLY: *(Into the phone)* Hello, Polly, it's me. DON'T HANG UP!!!
(Too late, Polly's hung up) SHIT!!! You little fuckin' ingrate!

(Light comes up from off indicating that someone has arrived home at the adjacent apartment. MOLLY *erupts, discarding the cellphone. She looks out the window, then rushes across to the exit door and whips it open. She runs out [Into the hall] and we hear her shout.)*

MOLLY: ARLENE!!! THEY'RE HERE!!!

(She waits a moment but ARLENE'S *gone.)*

MOLLY: Shit!!!

(She rushes back in, slamming the door behind, and crosses to the window. She assumes her shooter's stance, nervously positioning the gun.)

MOLLY: *(To herself, with quiet, desperation)* O K, boys, stand still... Shit! Where'd he go?... Uh-oh, the one guy's packing his bag...flying the coop. Gotta clip their wings. But I can't get...them both...SHIT! There he is. They're arguing. Now, if they'd just...get in a fight...wrestle around...one target, two shots... Oops, now the other one has a suitcase. These boys are ripe for elimination. If I could just get... both of them in my sights...come on, boys...a little closer...there we are. *(Starting to nervously squeeze the trigger)* Say goodbye, boys. *(She can't bring herself to pull the trigger. Shuddering...)* I can't...miss this...opportunity. If it's not them...then it's me. *(Unable to fire)* I can't...I just can't.... *(Distraught, she sits on the floor and reflects).* Jesus, I just signed our death warrant. These creeps will live and we'll die... Cause I couldn't...pull the fuckin' trigger. *Arlene* will kill *me*, now. Save The Boss the trouble. *(Back to the cellphone, she dials)* Hello, Holly? Was that your sister that just hung up on me? ...I'm sorry. I didn't know you were on the other line. You're not the ingrate.... O K, "fuckin'" ingrate. It slipped out. It wasn't directed at you. Don't do as I say, do as I do. *(Her hand on the rifle)* Well, don't do as I do, either.

Why does Polly always hang up on me?... She doesn't *hate* me! She just *says* she hates me... SHE DOESN'T MEAN IT!!! You have to *know* someone to hate... Yes, like I know your father... Do *you* hate me?... Good, keep it that way. How come you don't hate me like Polly does?... Oh, great. Just the answer I needed to hear. Does that mean *you'll* hate me when you're her age?... Promise?... I love you too, Holly. *(Trying to compose herself)* I'm at work.... A new job...I work for an exterminator.... No, not in an office. On site...in the field...I dunno. I picked it up. From rats I've known. I specialize in rats. Male rats. No, it's not "icky" in the least. It's fulfilling.

Is Charlotte still there? "Charlotte The Harlot"? ...I'll call her whatever I want! Are you warming up to this slut? I'm your mother. She's not!!! Remember that! *(Defensively)* O K, O K. Sorry, sorry, sorry! Just don't hang up! I hate it when people hang up on me. I'm sorry I said it. You're right, I don't even know her. But I know HIM... Is he gonna marry her? Well then, she shouldn't be there with you girls. A bad influence. My lawyer's assured me, I'll have you soon. Not some stranger. I'll be able to afford you guys,

soon. Exterminating's lucrative... Uh, it means "profitable". It means I'll
be rich. So, don't go getting attached to this "Charlotte The—" ...uh, to this
"Charlotte".

*(The light goes out on the wall so the opposite apartment's been vacated. She peers
across, then sags at her predicament.)*

MOLLY: I know you're only nine years old.... I wanna tell you about men...
Yeah, boys. Unfortunately, boys become men... Yeah, sure you know that.
    I fear for you. I almost wish you'd follow your Aunt Louise. Nuns don't
have it so bad.
    If you ever fall in love...and marry...well, someday he'll come home with
the smell of another's love on him. That's when you leave... You'll know
what I mean when it happens. Excuse yourself! Pronto! You buy into
some guy's bull and that's the beginning.... Of *the end*, that's what it's the
beginning of. The end.
    I think you're old enough now to understand. Well, *understand* is not the
word. Who understands cruelty? Who understands why you're treated
like pond scum after you've given him everything? Look, I decided to tell
you this since, well... since you may not hear from me again... Easy, easy,
RELAX!... "Forever"? Who knows "forever?" Forever's a long time. For
awhile, maybe. I may be preoccupied. This job involves travel. Y'know, like
the Pied Piper of Hamlin...we'd read at bedtime. Anyway, I feel compelled
to tell you...here's how it was between us. *To hell with what he says!* I had
to go away *after* her. DID HE TELL YOU THAT??? *(Beat, apologetically...)*
Oh baby, don't cry. Please. I love you so... He lied. I didn't go away and
then Charlotte came into the picture. She had been in the picture for
months. *Our picture*. The fact is that Charlotte had to seduce Daddy so
that he'd defend her husband... "Seduce"... Ask your sister. By now, she—
...Never mind. Anyway, Charlotte and Daddy hit it off. So they got her
husband convicted. But he'll be out in a couple of years and, well...hell to
pay. But not to worry. I'll have you guys by then... Hey Holly, don't cry.
I didn't mean to— ...JESUS!!! *(Obviously, the daughter has hung up. She stares
at the phone, then addresses it.)* And HE named you girls "Polly" and "Holly".
Not ME! He thought it would be cute: Molly, Polly and Holly. But he thinks
Charlotte is cute, for Chrissakes!!! *(She lowers the phone and sits against the
wall pondering her fate.)*

(Fadeout)

Scene Two

(In darkness, we hear the buzz of an apartment intercom.)

(Lights slowly come up on MOLLY *asleep in the same position. A longer buzz and she stirs awake. Then she semi-panics as she tries to determine the origin. A third buzz alerts her to the intercom near the door. She rushes across and answers.)*

MOLLY: Who is it?

ARLENE: *(V O)* Who is it??? *(Thinly disguised)* "It's Angelina D'Arcangelo, you shanty Irish bitch! Mrs Tony D'Arc. I've come t'rip your tits off!"

(Angrily, MOLLY *hits the admission button. She recrosses, looks out the window then picks up the rifle. She holds it at her hip, her finger on the trigger.* ARLENE *enters carrying a pizza box. She stops, slack-jawed.)*

ARLENE: Easy, hon. It's me, Arlene. Your friend.

MOLLY: Get in here. Close the door.

ARLENE: *(Closing the door)* Chill, babe! I was only kidding about Angelin—

MOLLY: I'm not laughing.

ARLENE: No, you're not. But I respect your vigilance. It's paramount in this game. If you shoot me though, you'd have The Boss *and* the cops on your ass. But you're too intelligent for that. You're so smart I'm gonna commend you to The B—

MOLLY: What's in the box?

ARLENE: What d'you think's in the box? A flat-screen T V?

*(*MOLLY *indicates the table.* ARLENE *places the box.* MOLLY *indicates with the rifle for* ARLENE *to open.* ARLENE *does so but carefully making sure she opens the box with the lid against her mid-section.)*

MOLLY: What kind?

ARLENE: The works. Large.

MOLLY: The anchovies are yours.

*(*MOLLY *approaches and leans in to get a piece.* ARLENE *surreptitiously draws her pistol from behind the lid and holds it flush against* MOLLY's *forehead.* MOLLY *freezes.)*

ARLENE: God, you're stupid. Put the rifle down.

MOLLY: *(Nervously complying)* I wasn't gonna shoot. Honest! If you shoot me then you'd have...uh, you'd be in trouble.

ARLENE: *(Laughing)* With who? The police? *(Laughing harder)* The Boss?

MOLLY: If I was gonna shoot, I'd have drawn a bead...caught you in the cross-hairs...

(She mimes the phantom rifle to her shoulder, peers down the barrel and pulls the trigger with a quiet...)

MOLLY: Bang.

ARLENE: In your dreams.

MOLLY: You have the first piece.

ARLENE: I ate.

MOLLY: Ate what?

ARLENE: Steak.

MOLLY: *(Indignantly)* You had steak and you bring me anchovies??? Never mind. I pass. You may have poisoned the pizza.

ARLENE: If I poisoned you, I'd have ordered "plain". Small. Look, we gotta get together on this. After all I've done for you—

MOLLY: Done *for* me???

ARLENE: We need each other. Why'd you take so long to answer? I thought they got you. *(Putting her gun away)*

MOLLY: I was napping.

ARLENE: You were asleep at the wheel.

MOLLY: Assassinating is tedious.

ARLENE: *Waiting* is tedious. The deed itself is a rush. It's like fishing.

MOLLY: Fishing? A rush?

ARLENE: Well, like deep sea. Big time.

MOLLY: Where'd the gun come from?

ARLENE: I'm on duty.

MOLLY: *(Incredulously)* You're on duty. Where's your uniform?

ARLENE: I'm not some flatfoot pounding a beat. I'm a detective. *(Flashing her badge, briefly)*

MOLLY: *(Shakes her head)* My taxpayer dollars at work. How was class?

ARLENE: I'm feeling very ambivalent. These police cadets, they're so innocent. No concept of crime...or it's changing nature. They're all... like T V-influenced. They'd never suspect *me* of murder.

MOLLY: Should they?

ARLENE: Certainly! Suspect *everyone*. Any citizen is capable of the most heinous crimes. I almost feel like confessing to them. If they knew that I was a killer they'd be wary of *anyone*.

MOLLY: Suit yourself. But don't confess *for me*. I don't feel guilty...yet. God, I hated confession.

ARLENE: You? What did *you* confess to?

MOLLY: The usual. Sex, primarily.

ARLENE: *(Curious)* Whew! I never would've thought... You were a hooker?

MOLLY: Of course not!

ARLENE: Well, what'd you confess to?

MOLLY: Breaking the sixth commandment.

ARLENE: To the cops???

MOLLY: To the priest!

ARLENE: Ohhhhh, gotcha. Catholics...weird.

MOLLY: "Weird"? No more weird than—

ARLENE: I mean they'll disregard their civic duty to confess. But they'll confide their darkest secrets to a pederast.

MOLLY: Not all priests are—

ARLENE: *(More or less to herself)* And they call that "religion". By the way, adultery is the Seventh Commandment.

MOLLY: The Sixth.

ARLENE: The Seventh.

MOLLY: THE SIXTH!!!

ARLENE: THE SEVENTH!!!

MOLLY: SAYS WHO???

ARLENE: KING JAMES!!!

MOLLY: BIG DEAL, WHAT DO KING'S KNOW???

ARLENE: WHO'S *YOUR* SOURCE???

MOLLY: GOD!!!

(ARLENE shakes her head in despair.)

ARLENE: Well, as I said, those police cadets would never see *us* as hitters. Or those two across the way.

MOLLY: That's how we got the gig. We're anonymous.

ARLENE: I'd call us inconspicuous. That's like anonymous...but with class. *(Indicating the targeted apartment)* Nothing, huh?

MOLLY: Nah. I mean, they were here but—

ARLENE: Here???

MOLLY: *(Pointing)* There!

ARLENE: I thought you said—

MOLLY: They came...and went.

ARLENE: You *let* them?

MOLLY: *(Peeved)* They never asked my permission!!!

ARLENE: *(Angrily)* You were supposed to drill 'em.

MOLLY: I needed help.

ARLENE: TO FIRE A SHOT?

MOLLY: *Two* shots.

ARLENE: You don't need help to shoot. I saw you at the range. That's why you're here.

MOLLY: I had the one in my sights. But if I fired, the other guy could've shot *me.*

ARLENE: Uh-uh! From my considerable experience, the other guy freezes.

MOLLY: What if he doesn't?

ARLENE: He will. Shooters are cowards. That's why we shoot people in the back. And cowards freeze. So, you should've drilled 'em.

MOLLY: Easy for you to say. You were safe in class. Law Enforcement class, no less. A rock-solid alibi.

ARLENE: If I had an alibi why would I come back here? And with a pizza?

MOLLY: To eliminate the evidence. Namely me.

ARLENE: Damn, Molly! I brought you aboard cause we're pals.

MOLLY: Answer me this. Does The Boss pay *you*, then you pay me?

ARLENE: IRRELEVANT NOW! THEY'RE GONE. GONE FOREVER.

MOLLY: Like I say, nothing lasts forever.

ARLENE: Least of all, *us.*

MOLLY: Maybe they're sitting there in the dark.

ARLENE: Why would they do that?

MOLLY: They could be watching us.

ARLENE: We're supposed to be watching *them. (She pulls her gun.)*

MOLLY: They're *voyeurs?*

ARLENE: More likely, they've left town. For good. That means we blew the assignment. That means *we're* the hunted.

(She puts the gun to MOLLY's *head.)*

MOLLY: *(Nervously) The one guy's cute.*

ARLENE: Helllllooooo...ARE YOU ON THIS PLANET? *(Steamed)* I really dunno if you're cut out for this.

MOLLY: THAT'S NOTHING TO BE *ASHAMED* OF!!!

ARLENE: BUT IT'S SOMETHING TO BE *SCARED* OF!!! *(Suddenly, an idea and she sets out to open her laptop with energy. It has a N Y P D logo.)*

MOLLY: What now? What are you typing? I'm not saying anything that can be held against me.

ARLENE: Jesus, I don't *want* you to say anything. Ever.

MOLLY: Oh, now you're playing the cop with me. Hang the rap on Molly.

ARLENE: What rap??? We haven't shot anyone. Now settle down. If we don't have unity, we've got nothing.

MOLLY: Unity? Is that what we've got?

ARLENE: *(Pulling out her traffic ticket booklet)* Thanks to me, we've got something better. When I left for class, I ticketed their car.

MOLLY: You were an off-duty detective.

ARLENE: I know, but...I'm a cop twenty-four/seven. And they were in a loading zone.

MOLLY: You ticketed two guys you're gonna kill?

ARLENE: They won't have to pay the fine.

MOLLY: Have you no compassion?

ARLENE: I have compassion!!! I sponsor a foster child in Angola. I no sooner ticket the car when they come out and tear the ticket up.

MOLLY: Hey, that was your chance to drill 'em!

ARLENE: For a traffic ticket?

MOLLY: *(Beat)* And littering.

ARLENE: In broad daylight, huh? No, I got their license number and my police laptop. Voila! I'll punch up the license and the computer tracks their travel.

MOLLY: But what if they park at the airport?

ARLENE: We track their flight. If they go to Vegas, The Boss sends us out. Big per diem. We can hang out at the Bellagio before we ice 'em.

MOLLY: Arlene, you're a genius.

(*They slap palms.* ARLENE *types in the license plate.*)

ARLENE: This'll take some time.

MOLLY: I can wait. Hey, call up their I Ds.

(ARLENE *mouses up their quarry.*)

MOLLY: That's them alright.

ARLENE: Which is the cute one?

MOLLY: You don't know?

ARLENE: It's relative.

MOLLY: Oh. (*Pointing*) That one.

ARLENE: Barry Connelly. Librarian in real life. I suppose you want his phone number.

MOLLY: What for? He's not home.

(*They laugh gleefully.*)

ARLENE: Maybe they're gay.

MOLLY: What? Gay shooters? G'wan!

ARLENE: If there are girl shooters, there must be gay shooters. There are gay cowboys.

MOLLY: Oh, and I nearly forgot. The landlord came in.

ARLENE: To their apartment?

MOLLY: To *our* apartment.

ARLENE: (*Panicky*) He saw the rifle?

MOLLY: Yeah, but it's O K. The Boss owns the building. The janitor is a shooter, himself. Between gigs. He was pissed. He thought this should've been *his* score.

ARLENE: Too obvious. The accusing finger...

MOLLY: That's what I told him.

ARLENE: And it's not *our* apartment. God forbid, I should live *here*...and with you.

MOLLY: You needn't get bitchy, Arlene. As you suggested, we're in this together. There's no point pissing each other off. Not with this weaponry lying around.

ARLENE: Are you threatening me?

MOLLY: No, but I'm warning you, I have a short fuse.

ARLENE: Still? You never put a lid on your temper? After all these years?

MOLLY: It's gotten worse.

ARLENE: I didn't think it could have.

MOLLY: I have more to be pissed at now.

ARLENE: Have you considered therapy?

MOLLY: Have *you*?

ARLENE: I'm *in* therapy.

MOLLY: I should think so.

ARLENE: I could recommend you.

MOLLY: No need. A good shrink wouldn't need a reference to determine I'm bonkers. My behavior...back in high school, it was evident?

ARLENE: You were the only cheerleader ever thrown out of a game. For punching a ref.

MOLLY: He called a penalty on Anthony. It was behavior under the influence.

ARLENE: Of what?

MOLLY: Of love.

ARLENE: *(Amazed)* God, you really...

MOLLY: Yes. Yes, really...

ARLENE: Tony was your first, then

MOLLY: And my last.

ARLENE: Then how do you account for your two kids by...your husband... I presume?

MOLLY: Oh, there were plenty after Tony. But there was only one Tony.

ARLENE: *(A la Groucho Marx)* Now there's enough Tony for two Tonys.

MOLLY: I will always see him as he was at seventeen.

ARLENE: Geez, you're making me feel...well, real guilty.

MOLLY: (*Genuinely threatening* ARLENE) If it hadn't been you it would have been someone else. But it wasn't someone else. It was you. And you were nothing special.

(*Before* ARLENE *can counter, the computer erupts...*)

COMPUTER VOICE: The license plate you've entered is invalid.

ARLENE: Shit!

MOLLY: It's... phoney?

ARLENE: You bet. Those insidious bastards.

MOLLY: Well, send out a bulletin. Have 'em arrested. Tell your buddies to be on the lookout for *this* car...*this* plate.

ARLENE: Won't do any good. They haven't done anything wrong! They blew the assignment. Remember?

MOLLY: Hmmmm...hey, driving with phony plates!

ARLENE: We don't want them in jail. They could rat out The Boss.

MOLLY: If The Boss gets pinched, what would happen to us?

ARLENE: He'd rat *us* out.

MOLLY: Not much allegiance in this game.

(*The light from the apartment under surveillance comes on. The women leap to action. In the next few lines they pass the rifle back and forth like a hot potato.*)

ARLENE: They're back! Drill em!

MOLLY: Why me?

ARLENE: You're the expert.

MOLLY: Bitch!

ARLENE: (*Peering*) Shit!!!

MOLLY: (*Peering*) It's not *them*!

ARLENE: (*Peering*) Geez, Bonnie and Clyde.

MOLLY: Hardly. They're homely as sin. Not like in the movie.

ARLENE: They're looking right up here.

(*They back away from the window.*)

MOLLY: Then they've been sent to...

ARLENE: ...kill us. A co-ed hit team.

MOLLY: Bound to happen. Women shooters, gay shooters, co-ed shooters. What's next, tri-sexual shooters?

ARLENE: What's a tri-sexual?

MOLLY: I dunno. But I'm sure they're out there.
Hey, I gotta cramp in my trigger finger. Kill 'em while they're setting up.

ARLENE: Not me! I'm the brains, you're the enforcer. Lemmee massage your finger.

(The light goes out.)

MOLLY: They've left.

ARLENE: Nope. They just turned the lights off. They're sitting there waiting...for us.

MOLLY: For us to turn the lights on.

(They edge away from the window and try to relax.)

MOLLY: What now?

ARLENE: I'm prepared. I've got a plan B. You?

MOLLY: I've never even had a Plan A. What's yours?

(On all fours to dodge the shooters, ARLENE crawls to her purse. MOLLY follows.)

ARLENE: I'm ready to take off.

MOLLY: Well, I'm not one to stay put. Especially given the circumstances.

ARLENE: *(Digging for something in her purse)* Awhile back, we arrested a guy and he fell for me.

MOLLY: In jail?

ARLENE: That's where we put arrestees.

MOLLY: Don't let it go to your head, Arlene. Pickings are slim in j—

ARLENE: Jail. I know. Slim. He was doing ten-to-twenty. But he said if I'd help spring him he knew of a hidden treasure.

MOLLY: Who is this guy, Captain Kidd?

ARLENE: He gave me a map. *(Producing a handmade map after dumping the contents, i.e., handcuffs, Tampax, lipstick, keys, etc)*

MOLLY: You can get a treasure map on the internet.

ARLENE: This is real.

MOLLY: *(Cynically)* Forget what I said about smart women.
This treasure—

ARLENE: Loot!

MOLLY: How does your boyfriend know it's there?

ARLENE: He put it there. And he's not my boyfriend. I wouldn't fall for a lifer.

MOLLY: I thought you said ten-to-twenty.

ARLENE: After he gave me the map, I turned him in. My duty as a cop.

MOLLY: And not a very romantic one. (*Examining the map*) Hey, is this an original?

ARLENE: Damn right. I don't want copies floating around.

MOLLY: But *he* might've made copies. If there are multiples, the treasure's long gone.

ARLENE: Why would there be multiples?

MOLLY: This could be a scam. By the Chamber of Commerce.

ARLENE: Why would the Chamber of Commerce —

MOLLY: Tourism. If they distribute enough of these phoney maps—

ARLENE: My source *hardly* worked for the Chamber of Commerce.

MOLLY: Maybe he's from the town. Maybe his mother runs a B & B.

ARLENE: I doubt if he's ever had one.

MOLLY: A B & B?

ARLENE: A mother!

MOLLY: Well, we've gotta go somewhere, fast. (*Indicating the map*) This place is a start. Found loot. American enterprise in action.

ARLENE: How much money do you have?

MOLLY: Hardly anything.

ARLENE: Plastic?

MOLLY: I can't get any.

ARLENE: *Anybody* can get plastic.

MOLLY: I'm a bad risk

ARLENE: Tell me about it. (*Preparing to leave*) I'm going to the A T M machine. The map, please.

MOLLY: (*Grabbing the rifle*) Nothing doing. I will not be left alone here to stew in my own juices.

ARLENE: Good metaphor, Mol.

MOLLY: I minored in English.

ARLENE: Where?

MOLLY: Immaculate Conception College. After public high school and Tony D'Arc, my parents figured—

ARLENE: By then it was probably too late for Catholic rehab.

MOLLY: It's always too late for Catholic rehab. It's like seeking help from the source of the problem.

ARLENE: C'mon, let's hit the money machine and then we're off.

MOLLY: You get the cash. Then come back. I need time to clear my head. No wisecracks!!! *(Threatening)* Go!

(ARLENE nods then cautiously departs. MOLLY sits for a long moment on the verge of tears. Then she takes Tony's card from her pocket, places the pieces together on the floor, gets out her cellphone and dials. In a moment and in a quiet, nervous voice...)

MOLLY: Hello, Tony? It's... It's... Take a guess. I'll give you a hint... From high school... No... No... Good God, no! Geez, Tony. It's Molly... *(Anguished)* The only Molly in our class, FOR CHRISSAKES! ...Right! "Murphy". You're still sharp as a fuckin' tack! ...I'm fine, not that you seem to care.... Not any more. I'm sort of on marital hiatus... Yeah, two... nine and twelve...I agree. They're not what they were cracked up to be. So, you're working at a car wash? ...*Managing.* Excuse me. Somehow I figured that at this point in your life— ...You did too, huh? Understand, car washes are essential. Nothing to be ashamed of. But you had a football scholarship... So, why didn't you finish? ...I wasn't there to write your papers any more. Remember? ...I'M NOT THE BLONDE! I'VE NEVER BEEN BLONDE!!! *(Alter the line —if need be—contingent upon the actor's hair color.)* ...I'm not so sure, Tony. I'm not so sure you're joking. *(Beat)* Are you happy? ...What does "relatively" mean? ...Do you wanna get together? Talk? Y'know, just for old times sake? ...I could drive out... That's very nice of you. "The Spotless Special...With Superwax." Complimentary. Swell. I *can* afford to pay. I'm doin' real well... Gee, great...I got it from Arlene— ...Yeah, at the reunion... No, I was busy. Would you have remembered if I'd been there? *(Angrily)* Am I just a *blank* to you, for Chrissakes???... How come you remembered Arlene?... WHAT? In the parking lot she gave you a... WHAT??? "It will all come back" when you see me??? Well, what if I've put on two hundred pounds, YOU FAT TUB OF SHIT??? ...What? ...You're *not* fat? ...Yeah, I use the computer. There's one right here.... Your web page? Yeah, *you'd* have your own web page. Gimme your address... T-O-N-Y-D-A-R-C dot com. *(In a moment the Bee Gee's theme from* Saturday Night Fever *comes up and voice-over, "It's Disco Tony D'Arc. Now watch my moves". She goes wide-eyed.)* Gorrrrrgeousss!!!! *(Suddenly she throws the phone across the room and slams the lid of the laptop. The music stops.)* MOTHERFUCKER!!! *(She paces and mumbles...)* How did this happen to me?? I come from a good family. *(Beat)* Well, it wasn't a *bad* family. *(Suddenly, she crosses and flicks on the overhead light. She crosses and stands at the window as a literal target.(Shouting)* WELL SHOOT, WHY DON'TCHA??? SHALL I TURN MY BACK, YOU CHICKENSHIT FUCKERS??? *(She turns her back to the shooters. Nothing)* DON'T WAIT FOR ARLENE! PICK US OFF ONE AT A TIME, WHY DON'TCHA??? *(But nothing happens. Disgusted, she crosses and turns the light off.)*

(The intercom buzzes. She crosses and responds.)

MOLLY: Arlene?

ARLENE: (V O) Yeah, I got some dough for—

(MOLLY buzzes her in downstairs. She returns to the rifle, lifts it off the tripod and turns to the door. She lifts the rifle to her shoulder and intently peers down the barrel. Then she reconsiders and runs behind the door.)

(When the door swings open, ARLENE enters cautiously, bills in hand. She crosses a few feet into the room then MOLLY slams the door. ARLENE whirls around to face the gun. ARLENE is uncharacteristically fearful as MOLLY lowers her aim to ARLENE's crotch area. Then she drops to one knee to get an even better shot. ARLENE instinctively covers the targeted area with her hands. But MOLLY struggles with the dispatch of ARLENE just as she did with the boys. When ARLENE determines the hesitation she throws the bills in the air. Emotionally drained, MOLLY puts the gun down and slowly crawls around starting to collect the bills. ARLENE approaches her from behind—while MOLLY is facing the audience— and draws her pistol. She cocks it and MOLLY reacts in frozen fear at the sound. ARLENE violently grabs MOLLY's hair. For a long moment, ARLENE contemplates a bullet to the back of MOLLY's head in true shooter style. Then she uncocks the gun, reholsters it and drops to her knees to help her mate collect the dough.)

(Fadeout)

END OF PLAY

www.ingramcontent.com/pod-product-compliance
Lightning Source LLC
Chambersburg PA
CBHW061306110426
42742CB00012BA/2077